Country Doctor

Country Doctor
The Story of
DR. CLAIRE LOUISE CAUDILL

Shirley Gish

THE UNIVERSITY PRESS OF KENTUCKY

Publication of this volume was made possible in part
by grants from the E.O. Robinson Mountain Fund
and the National Endowment for the Humanities.

Published by The University Press of Kentucky
Scholarly publisher for the Commonwealth,
serving Bellarmine College, Berea College, Centre
College of Kentucky, Eastern Kentucky University,
The Filson Club Historical Society, Georgetown College,
Kentucky Historical Society, Kentucky State University,
Morehead State University, Murray State University,
Northern Kentucky University, Transylvania University,
University of Kentucky, University of Louisville,
and Western Kentucky University.
All rights reserved

Editorial and Sales Offices: The University Press of Kentucky
663 South Limestone Street, Lexington, Kentucky 40508-4008

99 00 01 02 03   5 4 3 2 1

Library of Congress Cataloging-in-Publication Data

Gish, Shirley, 1931-
  Country doctor : the story of Dr. Claire Louise Caudill / Shirley
Gish.
        p.   cm.
  Includes interviews with Caudill and Susie Halbleib and the
playscript Me 'n Susie, by Shirley Gish and Claire Louise Caudill.
  ISBN 0-8131-2077-2 (acid-free paper)
  1. Caudill, Claire Louise—Drama. 2. Caudill, Claire Louise—
Interviews. 3. Women physicians—Kentucky—Drama. 4. Women
physicians—Kentucky—Interviews. 5. Country life—Kentucky—Drama.
I. Caudill, Claire Louise. II. Halbleib, Susie. III. Gish, Shirley,
1931-   Me 'n Susie. IV. Title.
PS3557.I793C68   1999
812'.54—dc21   98-20274

For Melissa

Contents

History is what people have said to me,
and what I've heard, that I must write down.
—Herodotus

Foreword

John Kleber

In the mountains of eastern Kentucky, a story is told about Alice Lloyd, scion of a wealthy Massachusetts family, that when she thought of leaving her work in the Caney Creek area of Knott County, an elderly woman said, "Stay on, stranger." And stay she did, for more than forty years, to improve the lives of the people. No one had to ask Claire Louise Caudill to stay. Her roots were firmly planted in Rowan County, Kentucky. Although she went away to study medicine, after she returned with her degree in 1946, she never thought of leaving.

Dr. Caudill had a calling. Frederick Buechner has identified a calling as the place where one's personal happiness intersects with the world's great needs. In the ensuing years, Dr. Caudill found much happiness in meeting the needs of local people. Among other things, she delivered more than eight thousand babies. Similarly, Susie Halbleib, a Louisville native, found her calling working beside Caudill as nurse and friend. Together they demonstrated that individuals can make a difference for the better.

Another woman must be mentioned, and that is Shirley Gish. The mountains of eastern Kentucky are replete with a chorus of women who have helped to mitigate the violence, isolation, and deprivations of a rugged land of strong values where the outside is suspect. Gish came to Rowan County and soon felt a kind of calling to understand why Caudill was so special. The results can be found in the following pages. In the end, Gish was both inspired and enlightened, but no closer to understanding what made this remarkable woman do what she did.

In the movie *Casablanca,* Rick, commenting on the work of Victor Laslow, notes that while many try, he has succeeded. Like Laslow, Caudill is a heroic figure who has succeeded in nearly all she has undertaken. It is seen in the health of her patients. It is reflected in the large hospital that sits west of Morehead's downtown, and it can be read about in James McConkey's *Rowan's Progress.* But Gish's work adds more because here

Dr. Caudill speaks for herself. Here, also, some of her many friends give testimony to the fact that, like Laslow, hers was the heroism of persistency.

For all of its excellence, *Rowan's Progress* was Dr. Caudill seen through the eyes of another. The play *Me 'n Susie* is different. When Gish decided she wanted to know what made Caudill and Halblieb so special, she employed the technique of oral history. Both women modestly objected that they had nothing to say, but the series of interviews found here says otherwise. They convey a modesty and wisdom that reflect a true calling. To round out the picture, Gish interviewed seven local people. The result is a valuable primary resource for those interested in a history of rural medicine and women's role in it. It also became the story of a whole town.

For Gish, it offered a technique known to Saroyan, Miller, and O'Neill, namely, to take true people and dramatize them. When Gish first met Caudill, she felt an overwhelming need to know her. But simple acquaintance was insufficient. Gish is an actress and playwright who knows that the theatre can be a teaching tool and that good drama is a great moral force. The portrayal of Caudill as a strong and independent person can reach and inspire young women to think of their potential. The history of Eastern Kentucky is resplendent with strong women who have served as role models in a society that tends to be male dominated and often repressive. With the meeting of Gish and Caudill, the one has brought the other to life in a way only the theatre can do. Doubtless her two presentations of this play did have their impact. One can see how it would inspire others to pursue a life of rural medicine.

Although Gish's play imparts the power of drama, it reflects its weakness as well. Only a small number will ever see this play. For that reason, Gish chose to publish the script with the transcripts of the oral history interviews. In this manner Caudill's inspiration will reach many more. She can now touch other lives beyond the footlights. In a way, she will always be with us, conveying the true humanity of medicine. Gish's book is also a tome for the oral historian. It shows another way the technique can be most useful. Rather than having the tapes relegated to some musty repository, the printed words tell us here that in the act of common duty lies the heroic.

Acknowledgments

I would like to thank the following, whom I now count as friends, whose great kindness made it possible to complete the play *Me 'n Susie* and this collection of oral histories: first and foremost, Dr. Claire Louise Caudill and Susie Halbleib R.N.; but also those others who agreed to be interviewed: Lucille Caudill Little; Jane Caudill; Ellie Reser; Sister Jeanne Frances, Order of Notre Dame; Dr. James Quisenberry; Robert Bishop; and Eldon Evans. At MSU Theatre, Dr. Travis Lockhart, Dr. William Layne, and theatre students.

I also wish to thank Dr. and Mrs. Ronald Eaglin, Lori Godby, Sonya Hess, Dr. Charles Holt, Anthony Jones, Keith Kappes, Dr. Janet Kenney, Dr. John Kleber, Dr. Henry A. Sauerwein Jr., Kay Stiner, Stephanie Thompson, Donna Woodall, and Thom Yancy. I am very grateful to the Helene Wurlitzer Foundation of Taos, New Mexico, which gave me two residency grants. summer 1993 to write the play, and summer 1995 to edit the interviews. I also want to thank the Morehead State University Foundation for its support.

Everyone mentioned above answered all of my questions and calls for help with patience and warmth. Without them, the interviews and play could never have been recorded or performed.

Introduction

Dr. Claire Louise Caudill has been practicing medicine in Morehead, Kentucky, for more than fifty years with her nurse, Susie Halbleib, at her side. Together, they set out to improve health care for the women of this region, who once did not seek a doctor until they were about to give birth or were dying of cervical cancer. Dr. Louise and Susie traveled into isolated and mountainous areas by truck, sled, horse, boat, and even on foot, sometimes staying for days at a time. In 1957, they built a small clinic in Morehead. They have assisted at the births of over eight thousand babies, and they have seen to it that these babies all received their first immunizations.

This book is a collection of oral history interviews plus the script of a one-woman play that I wrote, based on these interviews. It is not unusual for a stage play to be adapted from a book, but this book was assembled after *Me 'n Susie* was written and produced. After seeing me perform *Me 'n Susie*, two historians from Morehead State University requested permission to read transcripts of the interviews. They concluded that my conversations with Dr. Caudill, her nurse, her family, friends, and colleagues had an intrinsic value beyond the play and should be published.

In the area surrounding Morehead in eastern Kentucky, anyone whose roots are not from here is considered to be from "off." When I moved here in the fall of 1989 to teach speech and drama at the university, I was definitely from "off." As newcomers will do, I asked neighbors for advice about finding the best doctor, dentist, and haircutter. Everyone told me, without hesitation, that the finest doctor in town was Dr. Louise. However, they also warned that she wasn't accepting new patients, so I was out of luck.

Residents were then quick to point out that the hospital in Morehead was named for Dr. Louise. Although the Saint Claire Medical Center would seem to be named for that saint who cared for the sick, it is also named for Claire Louise Caudill in honor of her driving force in bringing that fine hospital into existence in the early 1960s.

I did not meet Dr. Louise and Susie until the summer of 1992. One day, feeling very ill, I happened to walk by their modest office building on Main Street. There were no cars in the lot, so I went in, fully expecting to be turned away. Instead, I was whisked into an examination room by a tall, slender, sweet-voiced lady in white. This was the famed Nurse Susie. "Well," she said, "this is your lucky day. Our first two patients today have canceled." A small, white-haired dynamo then bounded into the room. I was enchanted by the radiance of Dr. Louise's very being and immediately wished to write a play about her. This led me to explore her life of courage and dedication, and, in seeking ways to portray her magic, I was introduced to the heart of an entire community.

Morehead sits in the Daniel Boone National Forest in the northeastern section of Kentucky. It is a beautiful forested area full of hills and valleys. Until 1974, when Interstate 64 was built, this town was only connected to the outside world by narrow winding roads. Morehead now has over eight thousand residents, and when the university is in session, that population doubles. In a town that not so long ago witnessed frequent gunfights in its unpaved streets, one can only be amazed by the changes that have come about.

Today, Morehead has a large state university and a hospital of such note that it has twice (1993 and 1994) been recognized as the outstanding rural hospital in the United States by the National Rural Health Association. These two institutions employ thousands of residents. Morehead is also a tight community, where people pull together to make things better and where prejudices are put aside when trouble occurs. Many residents attribute the town's growth to Louise Caudill.

Many, many words have been written about Dr. Louise and Susie. They have received countless honors, but they take it all in stride. They have never sought any reward other than that their patients should enjoy good health. So when I approached them with the idea of writing a play about them, they were rather reticent. "We'll think it over this weekend," Dr. Louise said.

A few days later, she called to say, "Well, I guess we'll just give that a try." I had already read about her career in James McConkey's wonderful book *Rowan's Progress* (New York: Pantheon Books, 1992). I therefore suggested that we meet several times over the coming months so that I could record their stories to help me to portray her on stage. I hadn't the least idea of the winding road this inspiration would put my life on. Over the course of these many meetings, I came to love these two great women and became ever more convinced that a play about them might inspire others, especially the young women of eastern Kentucky.

The process became more complicated as Dr. Louise, Susie, and others began to suggest interviews I should do with friends and relations. I chose only a few people to interview, but Morehead residents are still telling me Dr. Louise stories. Many of my students are proud to be among

Louise and Susie's babies. One young man told me that, during a blizzard, his father used a blowtorch to melt the ice off Louise and Susie's back door so that they could attend his birth. And there are innumerable little Louise and Susie namesakes all over this area.

In 1995 Louise Caudill was named "Country Doctor of the Year" by the Country Doctor Museum in Bailey, North Carolina, and Staff Care, Inc. Her story was published nationwide. She was also interviewed by Connie Chung for a CBS documentary (which, however, was never aired, Chung and CBS having parted company shortly after the filming). On the occasion of her seventy-fifth birthday, August 19, 1987, a huge party was staged in Morehead State University's Button Auditorium. Planned by Ellie Reser, the event consisted of skits and songs about Dr. Louise and her babies. Among the songs was one for Susie. Sung to the tune of "If You Knew Susie," the lyrics included "Ouch, ouch, ouch, what a girl," signifying the thousands of children who have referred to her as "Susie Needle." Only 1,300 people can be seated in Button Auditorium. All of Dr. Louise's "babies" were invited to be there, so thousands had to wait outside before it was time to enter and sing "We Are Your World." Not only wasn't there a dry eye in the audience that night but there was no traffic on the streets of Morehead.

Dr. Louise glides through all of this attention with a glowing smile and seems amazed by the attention. "I only did my job," she will say.

Everyone I interviewed in preparation for writing my play talked about how Dr. Louise has affected her hometown. They spoke so easily that each of their interviews became a mini oral history as well. They were almost like the backup choir for the soloist. I felt that the integrity of their stories should not be broken up. Except for occasionally removing my questions (of which there were few), I have left their words as a running narrative. I wanted each interview to stand on its own and did not attempt to piece them into chronological order.

The fourteen interviews that follow were conducted between October 1992 and June 1993. Usually I visited my subjects in their homes in Morehead, armed with a tape recorder and a notepad. The transcripts of the interviews and most of the audio tapes (except those by Louise and Susie) are now in the Special Collections archives of the Camden Carroll Library, Morehead State University, along with early versions of the play and other research materials.

I believe that these interviews and then the play script made from them may serve as an example, for the historian or performance artist, of what can be done with oral history. Granted, there is no formula for writing a play, and the choices of material I made were based strictly on my own sensibilities about what I wished to bring forth. I wanted to make Dr. Louise live and breathe on the stage. Too often, tapes and transcripts are produced, then stored and forgotten. I hope that, as a book, this record is proof that research, although slow and painstaking, can also become a life-affirming adventure.

Interviews

Dr. Claire Louise Caudill and Susie Halbleib
October 17, 1992

With my tape recorder and a few notes, I went to the home of Dr. Caudill and Susie Halbleib on a bright Saturday morning. We sat in their tiny kitchen with coffee and, I think, a great deal of trepidation on all our parts. While most oral historians arrive for an interview with a written list of questions, I didn't. But I had many questions in my mind about what a life like theirs has been like. On that first morning, I began with family questions.

SG: *Are you anything like your father?* CLC: I think a lot like Dad.

SG: *How's that?* CLC: Well, he never said very much but just sort of plondered along in his own footsteps and came out with what he . . . SH: Well, he read a lot.

SG: *Your father was a banker?* CLC: He was a lawyer, too.

SG: *A lawyer, and he didn't talk much?* SH: It depends on the situation. He was always with a book in his hand. CLC: Not really in court. He was a judge most of the time, but he still didn't talk. He listened.

SG: *Do you find that you do that, too?* CLC: I believe I listen pretty good, don't you, Suz? Unless you get my ire up. Then, boy, look out!

SG: *Do you know when that's going to happen?* CLC: It's liable to be anything—if it irritates my insides and there may not have been a reason in the world to it. It's mostly feelings. I go by feelings. I don't go by sense.

SG: *Do you feel better after, or do you wish you hadn't?* CLC: I don't know that I wish I hadn't, but I'm sorry I did.

SG: *Would you say that your father was one of your heroes?* CLC: Yes. I don't know that I was striving to be like him, but, as I tell you, I didn't go by thinking.

SG: *[To Susie.] If you think back, can you see that your parents were a big influence?* SH: Oh, sure. I can see a lot of things. I do things especially like my mother. We had plenty of aunts and plenty of relatives. We were sheltered, let me put it that way. Somebody loved us.

SG: *Are you from Kentucky, too?* SH: I'm from Louisville. I went to high school there, Ursuline Academy, and then I went to the Nazareth College [clinical at St. Joseph Infirmary] for my nurse's training.

SG: *You always knew you wanted to be a nurse?* SH: Oh, yes, I was always going to be a nurse. I said it for so long that I had to do it to save face. Oh, I did everything. I dressed dolls up like nurses. I was always going to be a nurse, and I loved starched white uniforms. White starched uniforms, I really do. **CLC:** You could have been a P.E. major. I had white shirts all starched and wore sharkskin shorts. I think about that. I stayed with white. Not when I started out. I wore pink and blue.

SG: *What I've noticed in Kentucky is this wonderful "kin" system—that people don't want to leave their kin or family and want to stay with them.* **CLC:** I think that's true. **SH:** I think more in the hills. **CLC:** I was thinking of a fellow who called this morning. He had some pictures and they had been painted in 1840 and they're supposed to be, he thought, perhaps of my great-grandmother and great-grandfather, or somebody like that. And he wanted to bring them over sometime, and I didn't know anything about it. It is the Proctor side of my family my mother came from, and I just know very little about that side of the family. Of course, the Tolliver side has been played up a lot—the Proctors and the Tollivers. You know, the Martin and Tolliver feud.

SG: *Why do you suppose people make such a to-do about those violent confrontations?* **CLC:** People don't like anything to run smooth because it doesn't have excitement. Everybody likes it when something turns upside-down, when people do something mean. The world does, everybody is just tickled to death because it proves . . . I mean, people just love to hear that.

SG: *Why, do you suppose? Why do they feud?* **CLC:** It's the nature of us, I reckon. You have to have the good side and the bad side.

SG: *It sounds like the bad side is more interesting.* **CLC:** Well, it is for the world. **SH:** And I think it is true. You can talk about your relatives, but nobody else can!

SG: *I guess that the kin system and your allegiance to your own family is very strong. Is that why you chose to stay in this area?* **CLC:** Yes, I think so. But I think I was afraid to get out of it. I didn't like big cities. I mean, I liked just the way I lived right here. I liked the hills, and I liked what I thought would be a good way to live. Right here. And I didn't think you could do that anyplace else. And I still believe it. I like everything right here, and environment is awfully important, I think.

SG: *Environment—would that be family and friends, or . . . ?* **CLC:** These hills, everything, just all the things. **SH:** And your family. **CLC:** Oh, yes, they are really important to me.

SG: *You used to live on Wilson Avenue?* **CLC:** Right there at the top of the hill where the Huffmans live now. Lived there from a kid on.

SG: *That's the first house you remember?* CLC: No, we lived in lots of houses, but I only remember bits and snatches of other houses. Then my grandmother and grandfather ran a hotel. It was down on First Street, right across from what is now the freight station. It burned down. I don't know when it burned. I'd say early 1930s or 1920s or somewhere along in there.

SG: *What did they do? Where did they go?* CLC: Actually, they lived someplace else, but they lived there, too, and I had two uncles that helped. Uncle Herb died when he was very young, twenty-seven or twenty-nine. And then we lived down on Main Street for a few years, right next to the post office. That's where I sold my lemonade.

SG: *You sold lemonade on Main Street?* CLC: Yes.

SG: *How old were you?* CLC: Oh, I guess seven or eight, somewhere along in there. And we made mud pies. You could sell those, too. We'd put a real cherry on them.

SG: *Did you have satisfied customers?* CLC: Oh, we did pretty good.

SG: *Was it you and your brothers and sisters?* CLC: Oh, my brother helped some, but mostly me and a friend that lived down the street.

SG: *Did you make much money?* CLC: Oh, we had some nickels and pennies and dimes when the day was done.

SG: *And what would you do with the money?* CLC: Oh, we made us up a thing to do. We ordered clothes from Sears and Roebuck.

SG: *Really!* SH: I haven't heard this tale. CLC: We knew about this girl and her brother—I did tell you about this—well, anyway, they didn't have any money and they lived back way off up there where the school is now, up in there. And we thought that they needed some clothes. So we ordered her a coat and some shoes from Sears and Roebuck, but we didn't have enough for her brother.

SG: *So you and your little girlfriend got clothes for this girl. What was your friend's name?* CLC: Sidney Evans.

SG: *Is she still around?* CLC: Nobody's around anymore. Anyway, we took this stuff over there. She was just a little girl around town.

SG: *Did you ever think of giving her your own clothes?* CLC: No, we wanted new clothes for her. Well, we took the things over there, and we couldn't find the way back. It was getting dark, and we were scared to death. We ended up way up the top of Wilson Avenue trying to get back.

SG: *Did your mother know what you were up to?* CLC: Yes, she knew what we were doing. She even helped us a little bit.

SG: *Did you sell the lemonade to do this?* SH: Did you know that when

you sold the lemonade, or not till you got the money? **CLC:** Not till
we got the money.

SG: *Why, you could have used that money and gone and bought yourself
some candy.* **CLC:** We could go to Daddy's office and get stamps and
buy candy. We'd go up to the office, and his secretary would give us
postage stamps, and they'd give us candy for them. Didn't you ever have
any fun like that?

SG: *What kind of little kid were you?* **CLC:** Oh, we did everything. We
were very interested in knowing what was going on. We even had circuses.

SG: *In the backyard?* **CLC:** Actually, we usually had our circuses up by
Daddy's office. In the back. Now it would be right where Holbrook's
Drugstore is . . . back in there. The main reason for doing it there was
that the best character in our circus lived behind there. He could play
and make snakes do things—live snakes—and he'd go get 'em and he'd
have 'em there for the circus. He turned out to be quite an outlaw. His
name was Joe. I think he went out west or into the hills and nobody
could catch him and we never knew what happened to him. But he was
real nice. He gave me a cameo ring. So I thought he was an awful nice
guy. Well, everybody played with the snakes.

SG: *They weren't poisonous?* **CLC:** I don't know. I think some of them
were. I don't know one snake from another snake. Lord, I haven't
thought of this stuff in forty years.

SG: *What was your specialty in the circus?* **CLC:** Oh, we all did tricks.
Have someone stand on your shoulders. I was always doing flips and
twisting and turning, cartwheels. That was my position.

SG: *Didn't your mother dress you up in ruffles and bows?* **CLC:** We had
to dress up. See, I had an older sister, Lucille, and she always wore
green and blue, and I always wore red and pink, yellow—those colors.
And Mother would dress us all up in the afternoon and take us to Aunt
Dell's, and sometimes I'd get lost, or I'd see Roy Day and we'd get into
a fight. We'd do all sorts of rough things like that. We'd be all prissed
up—

SG: *"Prissed up." That's a wonderful word.* **SH:** Hair curled?

SG: *Did you hate that?* **CLC:** No, it was okay. I sort of liked it if you just
got dressed up and then that was all for an hour. I liked to look pretty
for a little while, and then that was enough. I didn't like just staying
pretty, but my sister liked that. **SH:** She still does. **CLC:** And then
my brother did, too. He always wore a coat. He liked coats and ties.
Me, I didn't stay very prissed.

SG: *Was your mother ladylike in social clubs and things?* **CLC:** They didn't social club too much back in those days. **SH:** Well, she belonged to the Circle at church.

SG: *Which church was that?* **CLC:** Christian.

SG: *Is that the Disciples church that has music?* **CLC:** Yes, they have music.

SG: *Do you still go to that church?* **CLC:** Yes.

SG: *Did you go to Sunday school?* **CLC:** I went to Sunday school. My grandfather just *knew* you would go to hell if you didn't go to *that* church.

SG: *You say the changes now [in medicine] are unbelievable. How are things now unbelievable?* **CLC:** When I was in school we had just begun to have EKGs, that is, electrocardiograms, and they had four leads. Now we have twelve. A lead is so you get the impulse from different places. So originally we had four different ways of doing that, and now there are twelve. But we didn't have much of that at all then. It was just sort of a beginning thing and, to me, that's just mind boggling to think that back in those days we didn't use one. We bought an EKG in about 1959 . . . along in there. And I took a course . . . **SH:** In fact, you took two courses in how to read it at the University of Kentucky. Oh, there was snow then, snow knee-deep, and you'd get stuck driving there. **CLC:** One night I never will forget. We didn't get there [Lexington] until about time the course was over. Then I took a correspondence course from St. Louis. We did that a lot, didn't we? [To Susie.] Took courses. A little bit here and. . . **SH:** Well, you couldn't be gone that long—gone to Lexington. You had nobody to cover for you back then. **CLC:** And you had to have that challenge. See, that was the important thing to me. If you were just working by yourself, you had to read. Now, Susie, she still reads. She's learned an awful lot of medicine. She can see when I'm making mistakes. And you'd need another doctor, too. **SH:** You sure do. You need somebody to consult. **CLC:** And we kept learning from the books we kept in the back of the car to read when we'd go out on deliveries. **SH:** We got a lot of reading done then. A lot! **CLC:** And that's so important—to keep up with what's going on. You've got to treat the whole body and can't know just one little angle. And, you know, it's a sad thing that people want to say to a doctor, "Well, I'm sick," and that's all they want to tell you, and you are supposed to figure it out. That's your job. They won't tell you if their head hurts or their back hurts. Well, a lot of that is changing now. They've read a lot about estrogens and what they'll do to you—

SG: *What would happen early, early on, when you were having to travel east into the mountains? What kind of territory did you cover? How* *far away?* **CLC:** Oh, I guess we'd go fifty miles in every direction. **SH:** We'd go to every county around Rowan County—Carter County, Bath County, Elliot and Morgan, Fleming County.

SG: *How would they get to you?* **CLC:** They'd come. They'd drive over to get us. **SH:** You're talking about going out and making deliveries.

SG: *Yes, how did they get to you to get there? I can't imagine that all those cabins had phones in them.* **SH:** Oh, they'd come to us—somebody, a relative—or they would go to the grocery store or a place like that and then somebody, the husband usually, would meet us there and would lead the way in his truck. Sometimes he'd take us in the truck if the road was real bad.

SG: *So you were walking into some unknown territory there.* **SH:** Oh, often. Often. **CLC:** We even went in a sleigh. Yes, a horse and a sleigh. That was an experience!

SG: *These were people you'd met before?* **SH:** Oh, yes, we always (or almost always) saw our prenatals before. We started with prenatal care. I mean, you had to have prenatal care.

SG: *Had they heard of that before?* **CLC:** No. **SH:** Not much. **CLC:** One that always stands out in my mind was this fella came in and wanted us to deliver his wife. Said she was due right away. We said, "Well, you have to bring her in first." He said, "Well, she'll deliver soon." We said, "If you want us to deliver her, you have to bring her in." And so the next day he brought her into the office. Now, this was back in the very beginning, back about 1948, and we checked her and she wasn't pregnant. Well, they thought we didn't have very good sense because she could outline the baby and show you its feet and everything. He thought she was, too. Anyway, she thought really she was pregnant. Now, we could have, easy enough, gone off some night about 3 a.m. on some long journey and find that we were delivering somebody that wasn't pregnant.

SG: *Maybe I'm thinking of movies where someone rushes in and says, "Doctor, doctor, come quick!" And you didn't even know them.* **CLC:** Yes, we've done such as that. **SH:** Lots of times. **CLC:** Once we got there and found a women who'd been in labor two or three days with only the baby's arm hanging out. **SH:** A midwife had been there, an untrained midwife. I want to stress that. But that's all they had.

SG: *Would they lose a lot of babies like that?* **CLC:** No, most of the time they don't lose babies. Occasionally.

SG: *Did you ever encounter a clash of folk beliefs and modern ideas?* **CLC:** Well, a lot of the women would be pretty drunk by the time we got there to deliver. They drank the alcohol, yes, for the pain.

SG: *Was there any clash with midwives or a woman's beliefs or . . .* SH: I'll answer that. A lot of times, if you delivered by forceps, people really thought this was a terrible thing and it is a lot easier on the woman in some cases, and a lot of people objected to that, oh, bitterly about forceps. CLC: And also that we would make you uncover . . . SH: Yes, and a lot of people didn't want you to uncover. We had a delivery table that we put on the bed; we carried it with us. Oh, we were weighted down. We couldn't begin to carry all that now. We took IV fluids; we took everything. Each of us had two big bags. You wouldn't believe how proper we were. CLC: Or thought we were.

SG: *Well, was it hard to persuade the women to come to town? They could have said, "Well, my mother didn't do that."* CLC: They'd just plain come. We said we didn't want them to be caught without someone to take care of them. Come in first, or we wouldn't go. SH: In other words, they had to bring them in before we went out. But occasionally this one would come and we would have to go anyway. Some people we'd never seen, such as this case she was talking about with the baby's arm hanging out.

SG: *Did the baby live?* SH: Oh, no, it was probably dead a day or two.

SG: *Did you lose many patients?* CLC: Now, statistics don't tell you anything, because if there was something wrong they'd go someplace else. And actually, in this territory with that kind of condition, you never really get the picture. I believe you can say that's pretty true. Now, if we'd run into a bad problem, Susie would go with them and take them to Lexington, so they'd die in Lexington.

SG: *Did anyone ever die that you took to Lexington?* SH: No. Well, we had one mother to die.

SG: *Really, in all these years?* CLC: And, oh, I know you shouldn't say that, but we sent her to Lexington. SH: No, but they sent her back because she wasn't in active labor, but by the time she got back she was and we delivered her and she had a tear in her uterus and it ruptured and she died and nobody could help that. But it was a really bad situation. The little baby lived, and we tried to get the mother back to Lexington, but she died.

SG: *I am amazed. Considering conditions, that in all those years you've been delivering babies since . . . ?* SH: Since 1948. Yes, but none of the mothers ever died that we took to Lexington.

SG: *How long did it take? I mean, there wasn't the interstate.* SH: There was a road. It's still there. Highway 60. And that took two hours. And the funeral homes had ambulances, but if you had to lie down, you went in the hearse. That was a regular routine around here. If you had to have an ambulance, the funeral homes would furnish hearses up until, oh, 1970. That was the case here. From 1970 on there was an ambulance service—the dogcatcher's van. People said if you didn't die of sickness, you could of dog smell. Well, I-64 came through here maybe in 1963. They were working on it because we were working on the hospital then. It was 1963 or 1964, we were working on the hospital. Oh, yes. Dick Carpenter. He got the ambulance service. Dick worked hard on getting that ambulance service.

SG: *What other things might people call you for? Or did you just take care of mothers?* CLC: Well, we got called for a woman who had pneumonia, but she really had a vulvar abscess. But they said she had pneumonia. SH: But they may not have known. She had a high fever, and back then if you had a high fever you must always have pneumonia, and that could have been an honest mistake. CLC: Well, we'd go a lot of times for heart failure. We did that all the time. They just couldn't breathe.

SG: *But could you get there fast enough?* CLC: Well, it all depended. Sometimes they'd call early enough. I remember the first one we had where we couldn't do anything. It was cardiac decomp. She was all swollen. Everything was swollen. She was sitting outside, and it was just a little after dark, and we had a flashlight. But in order to be able to get the fluid out, you had to be able to hit a vein, and I guess it was impossible from the word go. You could not see a vein. You could not see an arm.

SG: *She was sitting outside just waiting for you?* CLC: She was just waiting to die, I guess. Her husband was with her. SH: It's better to sit up. You can breathe better. So it made sense, her sitting outside. She felt better. CLC: But we couldn't see to do anything. Not much could be done. And we got up once at three o'clock one Sunday morning and we got there and they wouldn't let us do anything. Said they'd already had a doctor. SH: Heart attack. But we've had a lot of strange experiences like that. We used to see a lot of different things, like kids here in town would get chicken pox. You wouldn't have them come into your office because they're contagious. You'd go to the home to see them. And measles. CLC: Well, they had sense. Most mothers knew when a kid had measles or chicken pox. SH: But I'm sure many a kid caught measles in our office. We used to see a lot of children, a lot.

SG: *Were your patients mostly children?* SH: There were a lot of children. They weren't mostly children. We saw everything. But a lot of children. There are pediatricians here now. I don't know if I could stand that screaming now at our age. I don't know. We just had a lot of commotion around our office all the time. **CLC:** Oh, I got bitten on the arm one time. That child drew blood! Oh, he didn't want me to touch him. He caught me, and I wasn't very fast.

SG: *When people were dying, then they probably stayed at home. Was it like the hospice program now?* **SH:** Yes, family comes, church people ... **CLC:** Neighbors. **SH:** You were expected to die at home. **CLC:** Well, you knew you were gonna die. You know, back when we started, women were still dying of cancer of the cervix. Now, we've been around for a while and that's long gone. Then, they were young and, I mean, they would just be miserable. It really was so long and drawn out and they'd be sick for so long.

SG: *Did they know why?* **SH:** Well, when they got so bad off you could plainly see what the problem was and there wasn't much you could do about it. You couldn't spot it ahead of time. We didn't have Pap smears then, and well, Pap smears mean a whale of a lot. **CLC:** When they say those are not much good these days, why it just burns me up. They don't realize. And when you see something like that, you just don't realize ... **SH:** The horrible way they died and the pain ... **CLC:** And usually it was somebody that was way out in the country and had dirty sheets ... **SH:** Had nobody with them. Never had anything in their lives. **CLC:** Oh, it just cut you. What could we do? Didn't have anybody with 'em.

SG: *It must have torn you up to see that and know you couldn't ...* **CLC:** Helpless—and you didn't know when they would bleed to death.

SG: *I read in Mildred Haun's book that women in the mountains then were just used.* **CLC:** Just used, that's all they were. **SH:** I think life like that was fading by that time [1940s], but I think it was still true to some extent.

SG: *Do you think the roads getting better changed the isolation here?* **SH:** Oh, definitely. **CLC:** You just try to get there, back in those days.

SG: *How did you get back there? Did you have a Jeep?* **CLC:** No, we did not have a four-wheel-drive Jeep. Most people would pick us up. We'd drive our car to, say, someplace like a grocery store, and then they would lead us there. Some might have a Jeep or a truck, might have a wagon, or they might have a horse.

SG: *Did you ever ride in on horses?* **CLC:** Oh, yes, we did that up in Clay County. We didn't know how to ride a horse, either.

SG: *How did you carry all your supplies?* **SH:** We just carried a bag. We had that other stuff when we were going to deliver a baby. Then we carried our IV fluids and our table. One time we had a woman way out. The only person there was her husband and her little boy, and she was going to deliver a premature baby, and we were trying to get her out of there and she was bleeding. She had a placenta previa, which means that the afterbirth's coming first, and she was bleeding. And so we tried. Well, there wasn't any way to get that woman out of there. We put her between sheets and carried her out, the two of us, and the man carrying the bags. **CLC:** You know, just rolling up the blanket. **SH:** Yes, that's what we did. We carried her out. **CLC:** A 'fur' piece. **SH:** Yes, a long way. About a mile or so. Luckily, she was little, too. **CLC:** And then we got an ambulance, and the ambulance took the patient and me to Lexington to deliver the baby, and she got along all right. The baby was premature, but it lived.

SG: *Did many people try to name their babies after you?* **SH:** There were an awful lot of Louises and Susies. **CLC:** And a lot of people named them together—Susan Louise. **SH:** And then there were a few Claires, but not many people realized that Louise's first name is Claire.

SG: *Is that for any reason?* **CLC:** Nope, they just called me that. I didn't have anything to do with it. Or Weezer. Most of 'em couldn't say my first name, and the little nieces called me Weez.

Robert Bishop
June 12, 1993

Everyone who knows Louise noted that Mr. Robert "Bob" Bishop (born August 8, 1911) is her oldest and best friend. Mr. Bishop graciously invited me into his home, now on the campus of Morehead State University. His memories of what the town was like, of his family, and of his school days with Dr. Louise (he refers to her only as Doc) are almost a history of the town. His disclaimer at the opening of our interview—that he didn't have much to say—was then totally belied by this delightful narrative. There were almost no questions asked, and I am certain he has many more stories.

Bob Bishop is a man rich in memories and full of interests. He now raises Black Angus cattle and, as a former drug-store proprietor, has named his place Pharmacy Farm. His pride and joy, however, is his beautiful collie "Prince."

I'm not sure I've got anything that you can use or that would be helpful, but my connection with Louise is a longtime personal thing. From the first day I went to school, Doc and me went to school together. And in the same class—and I'm eighty-two now and my memory of things—well, I can't know people's names sometimes. People I've known a lifetime. But our teacher was Mrs. Hart. Now, why I remember Mrs. Hart's name—and I've had hundreds of teachers that I've known through the years and I had her only one year and I was only seven years old. Doc was six and I was seven. Got started a year ahead of me. But I never went to school until I was seven years old. I was fortunate that I was seven years old; I've always said that I was glad they didn't start me until I was seven because Louise and I were in school together and took the same classes. We took the same classes all through the grades and then, of course, that was the last year of the Morehead Normal School. Then for a year or two there wasn't any school there at all. So then, of course, Louise and I went to the public school. We stayed in the public school all through.

We stayed in the public school and graduated together. All those years, we took the same courses—except that she took sewing one year and I didn't take sewing. That's the only class in all those years that we wasn't in the same room. And, oh, 90 percent of the time, I'd say, we sat in adjoining seats. Of course, I went down to her home just like I went to my own home. We studied a lot together, you know, and I never—oh, you don't do those things now—but I never knocked on the door. I just went on in, and we'd go up to study. That is really my connection with Doc.

My father died the year I graduated from high school. In fact, Louise and I, we finished in the midsemester and then we went up to the university some. I took Latin and some of those subjects up there. And then, the night we graduated at the Christian church—that's where they held the service—my father died. I graduated and then he died that night. He was in the hospital in Lexington. He'd had surgery. He had cancer. He'd had several surgeries in Louisville and Lexington both. They told me right after the ceremonies. But then I entered the university. I was only nineteen years old. Of course, that's pretty old to enter the university now.

We were in the retail drug business. My father started that drug business in 1896 and then in 1930 is when he died. So I'd planned to go to a college of pharmacy. My father was a pharmacist. He didn't go to school. He studied and practiced under doctors. He didn't graduate from any college. You didn't used to then. Well, it was like lawyers. You didn't have to go to law school to practice law. You just studied under somebody and when you could pass the examination, you could get a license.

Anyway, I had one brother and two sisters. I'd worked in the drugstore as a kid. Oh, this has nothing to do with Louise. But it just gives you the background. But the reason I went in the drugstore, I worked in the drugstore—well, we were all born where the Doran student place is now [Adron Doran University Center]. That whole block belonged to my father.

My grandfather lived on one corner and we lived on the other corner. One whole block there, except for the jail, belonged to my father. We owned that. Then, after my father died in 1930, oh, two or three years later, my mother sold that to the state and then we bought a lot here [on University Boulevard]. This was all open country. Only one big house was out at the corner where Doctor Holbrook lived—none on Second Street. But all around here, that was just open field then.

I'd worked in the drugstore as a kid, and I worked with some friends that I'd gone to school with. My mother said, "You can work in the drugstore on Saturday and work all day, or you can work in the garden and work half a day." So I chose to work in the store all day, rather than work in the garden. And I later went into the farm business, and my brother, who did that farming, you couldn't get him on a farm, no way. And I ended up on a farm. That's just the background to it. Now, anything you want to ask me about Louise?

Well, we lived over here and she lived on Main Street. Let's see, her home was right across the street from where that building—a woman's furnishing store—across from that. My father's drugstore was down on First Street, right across from the depot. That property still belongs to me. We built that office building for commercial credit. Now that is Stansbury's office, CPA. That's where we started and then we moved to Main Street. The banks were there and the hotel was there, the old People's Hotel [the first three-story building in Morehead]. At one time some of her people owned [the hotel]. Some of the Proctors owned it. You know, she was a Proctor. Mrs. Caudill had two brothers, Herbert and Ezra Proctor. Ezra was a lawyer here. Herb was a businessman, and he moved away from here years ago.

We all played together, oh, yes! We did all kinds of stunts. We had plays. Maybe all kids do it, and we engaged in just everything that two kids do. It just seemed that when we went anywhere as kids, Louise and me generally went together and did that all through school. We went to all school functions together. As a kid, oh, she was one of these people who was in everything. She was active, you know, very active. She was somebody who was content with Louise. She was always, you know, a kind of a leader. She had that characteristic of leadership. And people liked to go along with what she did and with what she wanted to do. Things like that.

So then, after she left, you know she was gone for many years. Of course, when she came home for vacation, we'd be together. Now, that was back in the times when she knew everybody in the town and I knew everybody in the town. If you saw a stranger on the street, didn't nobody quit till you found out who they were and what they was doin' here. And you knew every family and you knew every kid in the family and you knew their names. You knew what their father did. That's what you'd get. I guess you had that in all small communities. But, you know, Morehead was just a wide place in the road. Why, I've seen trucks and cars get stuck right in Main Street of Morehead and had to be pulled out. In the mud, yes. We didn't have any streets. And when they finally started putting in limestone—we had the streets that crossed the main street from one side to the other—were made out of what is known as freestone. That was a big industry in this town for years.

I've seen three industries go through Morehead, through this county in my lifetime. And the freestone industry was quite an industry. Well, then, of course, it was a great lumber industry years ago. Clearfield Lumber Company came here. That was a group of men, Mr. Wrigley and Mr. Lee. Bill Wrigley. They were from Clearfield, Pennsylvania, and that's why they called it Clearfield.

So, these people came from Clearfield, Pennsylvania, and after they came here to locate a plant—there was a big band mill plant—they built the Northfork and Clearfield Railroad. And Snyder, a man from Pennsylvania, he was the engineer that built the Morehead, Northfork Railroad. Well, they cut out the timber and then—Mr. Lee had died by that time—and then they started the Lee Clay Products Company. That is a clay tile plant. That was operated by the same people, and they owned thousands and thousands of acres of timber land.

And then that's how the fire clay industry came into this part of the country. There were two or three big ones. Soldiers is the biggest. That was the fire clay that was used in locomotives and in the linings of steel furnaces at that time. And so we went through that. So we went through those three different industries just in my lifetime. Now we're back in the lumber business. And now I'm in the cattle business.

My father was born in Gallipolis, Ohio. He had a furniture factory, and they had a farm burn out and they moved then to Catlettsburg, Kentucky. Then the river flooded, and he lost again and went broke again. Then he finally came to Rowan County and made furniture and sold that and made things like caskets. Then you didn't have embalming. You had just funerals—undertakers, you called them. He had two big horses and a carriage and a hearse they drew. He had two big horses and he was all dressed up and drove those horses. Oh, I know Morehead from way back!

The famous pony story? Oh, yes, that was . . . oh, it was Eldon's brother, Drew. Anyway, the Evanses lived where the National Bank is now. That was Bill Young's home. The Youngs were very prominent lawyers. Bill had been circuit judge and Allie had been a circuit judge. Of course, Louise's father was a circuit judge and he defeated Henry R. Pruitt. So, after Bill Young died—he was killed in a railroad accident—after that, Mr. Drew Evans Sr. bought that house. He was a big timber man and he bought that house. We played a lot down there in that house. That was a big house. That was a great big house! They had a dumbwaiter from the basement up to the first floor. They cooked down in the basement, and they had a dumbwaiter, you know, that they raised up. And we'd ride that dumbwaiter up and down.

And Eldon's brother—oh, we were about the same age—and he was the one that took that pony up into that house, up the stairs, and up into that attic and it had a dormer window and he opened the dormer windows and stuck the pony's head out the dormer windows. Louise could have been in on it. That was the group we ran around with, played with.

Louise was very athletic. Played ball and all. Oh, yes, she was good. She was an excellent tennis player. You know that she taught physical education here and she played golf and she was real active. I never was much of an athlete. I never played high school basketball or football. The only sport I ever played, I played golf quite a bit. They didn't have a golf course here. We played golf over to Mt. Sterling. Then they closed that, and we went to Winchester and played golf for a year or two, and then for the last years of my golfing career we played in Maysville. Doc was a good athlete.

Now I call her Doc, but as kids I always called her Louise or Weezer. And she was my best friend. Oh, yes, we were close friends. I've said many times—I have made the remark—Louise, you know, has got a brilliant mind. She is a brilliant person and I used to say that she was smart enough to get me and her both through school. It was kind of an unusual thing, you know, she never married, and I never married, and we went to a lot of social gatherings together. And everybody thought when we'd go places that we'd generally go together. Our association was a very deep friendship. I've probably never had a friend I was as close to as Louise.

When Louise came back here, I said to her, "Why in the world are you coming back here to Morehead to practice medicine?" She'd been to school, you know. She'd been in school in New York and she'd been to school in Ohio State and she'd been in school at the Louisville College of Medicine and maybe even some other schools. And I said, "Laws me, of all those places, looks like to me you could pick some other place besides here to start practicing medicine."

And she told me this, she said, "Well, I've enjoyed the places I've been in the East, New York." You know, she's traveled quite extensively and now she's traveled worldwide.

So I said, "Why in the world are you coming back to Morehead?"

And she said, "Well, I'll tell you."

And I said, "Laws, there's a lot of disadvantages here."

And she said, "Yeah, I know that there'd be some of that in practicing medicine here. But in all the traveling I've done and in all the places I've lived, I could always find things that I didn't like. But I just decided that if no place was perfect as far as I was concerned, I might as well come back home and practice where I know the people. And that's why I came back home. There's a lot of problems here. There's a lot of problems everywhere! I'll never find a place there aren't problems, so I'm coming back to Morehead."

And she did come back from the day she started practicing. Of course, back then, there was a feeling about women practicing medicine—that is, about men going to them. But Louise and me had been so close that I just said, "Well, that's who I'm going to see."

Now, it was a funny thing. I'll give you this example of the feeling. I had a friend, a businessman, and he was a patient of Doc Louise's. He brought a prescription in the store from another doctor. And I said, "I thought you went to Louise." I was close enough to him and we were more frank, maybe, in those days, I guess. He had hemorrhoids and he had a prescription for ointment. Well, that meant he had to be examined for hemorrhoids, you know, and he said, "Do you think I could go to Doc Caudill?" And I said, "Well, I'm sure that's the way you feel, but I've told Louise that she's my doctor from one end to the other." I mean, it's a professional thing. And I just feel close enough to her.

So I never saw another doctor after Louise came here or a doctor that she didn't send me to. Now, I've seen neurosurgeons and I've seen other surgeons and I've seen a great many different doctors. I never went to one outside of general practice unless she'd say, "You ought to see a neurosurgeon" or "You ought to see this or that one." So I remember the first neurosurgeon I went to. I said to her, "Now, Doc, you be sure to tell him that all you want him to do is to examine me and decide what should be done. But I don't want any operation on anything. He is to report to you and then you decide what to do." And I remember this very prominent neurosurgeon in Lexington, long since passed away, but he said to me, "Well, I see that Doc Caudill and you have decided that you want my opinion and then you'll decide what I'm to do!" And I've done that all the time. I've never been to a surgeon or any other doctor but what she has sent me to.

Oh, yes, she has a very special feel for diagnosis. There's no question about it. I was in the drugstore one night and I had this hernia. It became terrifically painful. I called my sister and told her to call Louise and tell her to come down, I'm in bad shape. So, her and Susie came down. Finally Doc said, "Bob, we're going to have to take you to Lexington and you're going to have to be operated on and you're going to have to be operated on tonight." That was before we had the ambulance. The funeral parlor people was the way. They had the ambulance. So, her and Susie went with me to Lexington. And she had called Dr. Francis Massey, a prominent surgeon in this part of the country then. We didn't have as many surgeons as you have now. They went with me. One time I even said, "You've just got to stop until I ease this pain." So we went there and I was operated on that night. It was a strangulated hernia, and they had decided that maybe there was some gangrenous tissues.

Massey always said that Louise decided how much—he told me how much of my intestines I lost—he said that Doc Caudill, she was the one decided how many inches to do. I think that that was just a story, anyway. But you just don't have people do like that for you anymore. In fact, her family got all worried. She didn't come home that night and she didn't tell them where she was going and they didn't know where she was until she came back from Lexington. Course they left me down there.

Louise Caudill made a big difference in this town—in Morehead. Oh, yes. Certainly, as far as the medical function is concerned, there is no question. There'd have never been a hospital here. Oh, might have some time, but there would never have been a hospital established when St. Claire was established if it hadn't been for Louise. They can talk about all the people on the committee—I wasn't on it—but my brother-in-law, he was the county agent and was trying to raise some money for it.

Oh, I contributed to it, oh, yes, and my mother did, too. But there just wouldn't have been a hospital here, I don't care what anyone says. Oh, all of them was for a hospital. Oh, I guess Arvis Porter started practicing before they had a hospital, but I guess that was the only doc. Back in those days, see, when I grew up, there were two prominent families. They were all GPs then. We didn't have specialists here in Morehead. Dr. Grover and Dr. H.L. Nickels, they were brothers, and they were the prominent doc tors here. But they had passed away before the hospital. Dr. Atkins left there before they started the thing, and Dr. Jerett was living and was active. Everett Blair, Don's father, was here. Dr. Grover Nickels and my father were real close friends. He was my father's physician and Dr. Everett came and he was more near my age—older—but I went to Everett. Anybody that says to you that this hospital here, well, and don't know about Dr. Louise, well, she just organized it.

Now there was not a Catholic church here, and so she contacted the Methodists, and she contacted the Christian and the Disciples of Christ—that's where she goes—and the Baptists. She really tried to get a Protestant denomination in that hospital, but they just couldn't.

Oh, yes, there was some opposition. Back years ago, you know, the Catholics were looked at as a different type of people. Now, Emma Sample is still living, and she stayed with us. She had a room in our home out there when she was teaching. She was one of the original teachers at Morehead Normal School. That was a state school, and every Sunday morning she got up and got on the 21 C and O and she went to mass in Mt. Sterling every Sunday. Back then, the Catholics would also meet on Friday. Now to us we didn't see anything particularly wrong with her, I mean, with the Catholic faith. But the mountains were kind of anti-Catholic. It was Protestant dominated. It is still. She ran into some of that. You see, that's what Doc has that most people don't have. She could sell you a bill of goods, I don't care what it was. Why, you just couldn't figure out enough reasons not to do a thing if Doc was for it.

She's a great personality, you know. As I know her, and all I know she's

done and everything, she is still Louise to me. And we were friends long
before she started up in the world. And now, of course, every time she
gets an award I generally go when she gets it at the university, you know,
and it's just a personal thing with us. The fact that she has all these awards
and that sort of thing, it don't make a bit of difference to me in the world.
I generally go to those. And, of course, I'm in her office once or twice every
week, and on Sundays I go out to Louise's. We just sit there and talk and
watch the ball games and to me she's just Doc.

I'm sorry that I can't just say something to really tell you what I—all
I know she's done—it's unbelievable. Still, to me, she's just Louise. We can
just sit and talk and it doesn't matter what degrees she gets or what honors she gets. That doesn't put me where I can't talk to her. I can say anything to Louise that I'd say to anybody. I can call her any time.

And she came to the house when my mother was sick. Oh, yes, she
took care of all our family. She took care of Ed and Marguerite, my other
sister. She took care of Roy. She took care of me. Right today, if I was sick
there in that room, I am sure as we're sitting here that Doc would be here
to see me. You just don't have friends like that. You just don't have them,
that's all. Today, Doc Louise don't want to do any more practicing, and I
think she really wants to retire, but I think the reason she doesn't retire
is that there are just so many people that just. . . . Like I was talking to
my sister Roberta and we said, "Well, what in the world would we do if
Doc quit? What are we going to do?" And I've thought about it a lot. I've
thought, well, there's a lot of things liable to happen to me and there seems
to be a lot of things happening to me. I don't know where I'd go.

I've had no telling how many people say to me in the last few years,
they'd say, "Laws, if Doc quits, what are we going to do? I think that Louise
would quit today, but she just has all these people that look to her and
depend on her so much. She actually feels like she can't quit. She can't
leave them. Laws, I think of doctors I've known that started practicing
when Louise did and they have long since retired.

Doc, you know, she's like any of us who've gotten to the age we got
to. You don't do the things you used to do. She doesn't play tennis like
she used to. She used to play tennis maybe two or three times a week.
Basically, I think Doc's in good health for a person her and my age. I wish
I was in as good a physical shape as she is. She can't do what she wants
to, and she says she can't, and yet she won't retire. She won't retire as long
as she thinks she has an obligation. She just loves people.

I don't think there'll be another like her. When I was in the drug business, people were always asking me about doctors. And if anybody had
asked me about Doc Louise, I'd say, "Well, I'll tell you what. I think she

is one of the most brilliant people I know. And I think her knowledge of medicine is tops. I don't think she ever quit studying, and I don't think she ever quit keeping up with modern trends. If I had to recommend anybody, I'd sure recommend that you see Dr. Louise."

Today I'd say, "I don't even know if she'll accept you as a patient, but if you can get her, you'll win a prize that you'll always remember." Brilliant mind, brilliant. Heart of gold. Genuine. She's interested in the individual. She got a lot of awards and every one she got she deserved and if there's any more coming her way she ought to have them. But that didn't enter her mind that most people in town would think without her there'd never have been a hospital. That never entered her mind. That doesn't bother Louise. She's not looking for anything. I know that you could say, well, Doc's a wealthy person, and she is. Now, I don't know anything about her finances, but I know that she doesn't need the money. She sure wasn't practicing to accumulate any money, I'll tell you that.

Louise's and my friendship is just a different relationship. It wasn't just a relationship between a drugstore and a doctor, between a doctor and a patient, and I'm not sure I've contributed anything today about her. You know, I admire her ability. I admire what she's done, and I think she's a great citizen and she's done many things. But, to me, Doc Louise Caudill is a personal friend of mine, and I don't know how to tell about that.

With all the admiration, she's still just Louise to me. All her ability, things she's done, marvelous things. But to me she's still Louise Caudill. And when I see her tomorrow we'll talk about the things we've talked about for years and years and years. Her fame and fortune I admire, but it doesn't change my opinion. She's just my friend Louise.

Dr. Claire Louise Caudill and Susie Halbleib
November 7, 1992.

For the second interview I was again greeted warmly by both Dr. Louise and Susie. They said this interviewing was bringing back memories, and they were coming up with things they had thought were long forgotten. This time I had some definite questions about their education, and these led to Louise's thoughts on what teaching really ought to be. Perhaps the most moving words were in her description of her own doubts and fears about what she was doing and wanted to do.

SG: *What was your attitude toward learning, and what were you like in high school?* **CLC:** Learning was important. Yes, I'd say I studied pretty much, and I wanted to be the best in the class. I got to be valedictorian. But there was just nine of us! Math was my favorite subject.

SG: *What else did you do in high school besides study?* **CLC:** Oh, I was in all the things. You know, in a little school, if you have a debate club, or if you have a drama group, or whatever you had, you had to be in all of it, so I was in all of it. I debated. I was in all the plays. Can't say I was the star, but I was in most of 'em. One of them I had to sing in, and that liked to kill me because I can't carry a tune. Oh, I played basketball, but Mother wouldn't let me. But the coach thought I was pretty good, so we went to—this was a good experience—we went over to West Liberty—I think that's where we went—and, of course, I didn't have a uniform, and so I couldn't play. The coach said, "Now, Louise, if you were in there we could win this game." So I got a pair of knickers or something like that and put 'em on and played basketball.

SG: *Did your mother find out?* **CLC:** I told her. You see, I was supposed to be a lady, and I wasn't. So she'd try to influence me to not want to do things like that. I just wanted to do them. It didn't make me want to do them any more or any less. Finally, she came around and decided I could do whatever I wanted to do. There was no real turmoil over it.

SG: *If it was a class of nine, were you all close friends?* **CLC:** Oh, we had a big class in the beginning.

SG: *Was your social life centered around church?* **CLC:** No, I guess school as much as anything. We had a big class in the beginning. Not big in your numbers. You see, the Morehead State Normal School came about the time I was in high school. The State University came from a normal school and, you see, you could go up there in high school, so about the time I was a freshman in high school you could. They said all the girls went up there to find new boys and all the boys went up there to find new girls, so the nine of us stayed put. The school was right there where the Department of Education is now—Second Street. I could just run out my back door and be there after the last bell would ring. They tore that building down.

SG: *If you had only nine students, what did you have for teachers then?* CLC: Oh, we had one, two, about four or five teachers. They were divided up, you know, like teachers of math, a language, English.

SG: *So, even though you liked to play sports, you liked to study also.* CLC: I always liked to play sports. I liked to play tennis. We went up on the tennis courts when I was just a kid, usually with friends, but I played some with my sister. Usually with friends. Bob Bishop might have played some. I believe he did.

SG: *When you graduated from high school, what was in your mind to do?* CLC: Well, I thought I'd go to college, but I didn't have enough sense to know that you went to college to learn how to make a living. I didn't know that. [Laughs] My sister Lucille went through college before me and all she did was have fun—Chicago, New York. I just thought going to college was what you did to see the world (I swear that sounds awful), was like before you got ready to settle down. I believe I must have believed that because, well, you see, I *always* wanted to be a doctor. Always, always, since I first started going to school.

SG: *Had you known a family doctor that interested you or read books or* ... CLC: No. I think that Bob was going to be a pharmacist, and we were going to be a team. And my mother had a friend that was a doctor, a woman in Cincinnati, but I don't think I ever really met her, but I heard Mother talk of her, I would guess when I was six. Bob Bishop was the pharmacist. He was in my class. He was the one—I had to beat him to be valedictorian, and we went together and played together from the word go. In fact, since first grade we were in a dead heat to see who could be number one.

SG: *It strikes me as odd that you, as the woman, were the one who would be the doctor.* CLC: No, his father was a pharmacist. So he was going to take his father's place. So I was going to be the doctor, and that was as good as anything. We didn't know anything about it. He didn't know anything more about being a pharmacist than I did about being a physician. We went through every grade together—never wavered—until I went to college and didn't know what I was supposed to do. I can't imagine any college student being as ignorant as I was. I hadn't any experience. I hadn't. I was just a snot-nosed girl who just sort of played and nothing made any difference. I just did whatever I wanted to do.

SG: *Susie was saying she was always dressing her dolls, taking care of them. Did you play at doctor?* **CLC:** The way we played doctor, we got Castoria and gave out medicine. That's a laxative. **SH:** That's a good tasting laxative. They used to give it to children a lot. Foster's Castoria. **CLC:** Later on I took a bullet out of a dog's leg. The dog got shot and the veterinarian was old and he didn't want to do that kind of stuff anymore, so Bud went down and the vet gave him the stuff to shoot in it and somethin' to get the bullet out with, and on the back porch I did it. I guess I was fourteen or some number like that.

SG: *You must have had a reputation even then. Did your whole family know you wanted to be a doctor? Did they discourage you? If they didn't want you to play basketball, didn't they . . .* **CLC:** I don't think that. Basically, my mother thought women did not work. I mean, even though her mother was a milliner. Mother didn't think that women were supposed to work; thought that down in her insides. I feel sure that's true. But she wouldn't tell you not to do it.

SG: *What about your father? Did he encourage you?* **CLC:** Daddy said, "It's up to you, whatever you want to do." It didn't make any difference whether you were a woman or a man. If you wanted to do something, you could do it.

SG: *That was unusual then, wasn't it?* **CLC:** Well, I guess it was. But, well, an awful lot of women around here taught. I mean, you see, the normal school, when it came in, it involved women as much as men. Of course, you know the story of Cora Wilson Stewart, but I don't think they considered her a professional. I don't know if I'm saying that right or not. But other than teaching, I think that's about the story of women. I don't think there was anybody around here who was a nurse.

SG: *Who were the doctors here when you were young? What did people do when they got sick or broke a leg?* **CLC:** We had quite a lot of doctors. We even had an ENT man [ear, nose, and throat]. He and his brother did most of the medicine. Homer Nickel. And then we had a Dr. Blair. Not the Blair that is Don's father, but maybe his uncle or something like that. Then we had, after that, Dr. Adkins, and, oh, we always had pretty nice doctors. Nobody believes that because everybody says there weren't any doctors. That wasn't basically true.

SG: *So when you were a little girl, did you get sick and get taken to a doctor?* **CLC:** I had a leg ache when I was a little girl. Yeah, boy, and I think I complain about my legs now. We had Dr. Blair, and he used to come see me—they came to the house—and he brought this little black bag—it was about like that—and opened it up and there were pills on this side and pills on this side. All beautiful colors—pink, red, green, yellow, anything—and he'd point and say, "Now, which color do you want?" Well, I'd choose pink or yellow, and I'd take those pills and then the next morning I'd be fine. Mother would say, "Oh, you can't go to school this morning. You don't feel like it." "Oh, Mama, I'm perfectly well." And I'd be perfectly well and I'd go to school the next day. It was aspirin in different colors. I didn't know that.

SG: *What happened if people got shot or cut or needed their appendix out?* CLC: You had to go to Lexington. Lexington is where we usually went. The funeral homes would take you; they usually had an ambulance and they took you. I can't remember much of that, really. It took about two hours. Except if Drew Evans was driving. Then you'd get there just about like you do now. You remember I talked about Sidney Evans last time? This was her brother.

SG: *The one you made lemonade with?* CLC: Yes, and planted flowers. Oh, we did all kinds of things. Well, we'd plant zinnias. I think we had zinnias, going down the street—Carey Avenue there. Down toward the depot we planted them all along there one spring and had flowers. There was always a wide place, about a yard wide from the building to the street, and we just decided that it would look pretty. Oh, we had a great big playhouse—a pretty good-sized playhouse—and we'd go in there and cook and do things like that. But seems like we'd always like to get outside. Yeah, all of Morehead was a place to play; we played anyplace. Well, we lived right in the middle of town. We knew everybody in town, and everybody knew us and would tell on us. We'd do something and they would call our mother. "Did you know that your children were doing such and such?" So, in a small town, there's some good and some bad.

SG: *So let's go to what next. You finished high school and then went right to where?* CLC: Actually, I finished high school in the middle of the year, so I went up to the university [Morehead State]. I took courses in algebra, chemistry, and physics. I think that is all I took, those three courses. I don't know how I got out early. I just did everything you were supposed to, but I came out with enough hours at the end of the first semester.

SG: *So you knew you were going to medical school?* CLC: Well, yes, I sort of did. In the back of my mind I knew that's where I was headed for, and then I went to Ohio State in Columbus. Cille was there; my older sister was going there. She was studying music primarily. Music was really her field. I don't think she ever planned to teach any more than I did. But she did teach up here for a while.

SG: *Had you been out of Morehead when you were younger? Had you traveled?* **CLC:** Not a lot. Remember, it was 1920-something before we had a road out of here. We went by train. Well, I think I told you the other day that Chatauquas came through here and things like that. We had them as long as I can remember. Oh, and some had good mysteries and some good musicals, some comedies, some dramas. They were real good. See, as long as I can remember, we had a school here, and I think the school brought in lots of people you wouldn't ordinarily have run into. **SH:** You did get on the train and go to Lexington now and then. **CLC:** Oh, yeah, that was your shopping spree. The train would go down at six o'clock and at ten o'clock and come back at ten at night. So usually you took the six o'clock in the morning. Oh, we had a big time. We had breakfast on the train and everything, and then we shopped. I always kidded Mother that she went to Lexington and spent the day and came back with a tent shovel. That's what she called it. She enjoyed it. Most of the time she bought lots of stuff. I didn't like to shop too well.

SG: *So, when you were in college, what was that like?* **CLC:** Well, that's when I found out how smart I was. I went to see Lucille in a play one night, and this woman sitting next to me knew I was Cille's sister and she said, "Do you act?" And I said, "No." She said, "Well, you must sing." I said, "No, I can't sing." So she said, "Well, you can't do anything, can you?" Oh, college was fun. Of course, the first year we lived in the dorm, and we had two girls in this room and two girls in that room and a bath in between, and that's where I got into physical education. See, this girl in the other room was making a talk on how to serve a tennis ball, and she was a-workin' and a-workin' to serve a tennis ball, and that's when I found out you could major in that in college. So that's when I developed my major, physical education.

SG: *What happened to your early idea about becoming a doctor?* **CLC:** After I was through with school I threw all my books away—with school—I'd had it. That was on the 27th of June. July 4 I was going to New York to work on my master's.

SG: *Well, what happened in that week?* **CLC:** Oh, everybody else was going to New York to go to school. Lucille was. She was going to Columbia. And then the Brown girls were going, and there were nine of us had an apartment in New York on Riverside Drive and 116th. Did you ever hear of McCormick? Commissioner of corrections? Well, he was the commissioner of corrections of New York City, and we got his apartment. Well, he wanted to rent it, and his wife had gone up to Maine or something. Oh, that was a great experience. He sort of liked me, and he was always making talks places, and he'd take me along, so I heard him talk a lot of times. In fact, he'd bring some prisoners up to our apartment every now and then. He believed in probation and how to educate prisoners to do something, not just lock them up.

SG: *A couple of girls from Morehead, Kentucky, and a couple of prisoners sounds like an interesting evening. So here's a little girl from Morehead in New York City. How did you do?* CLC: Well, did all right every place but in school. I did come out with a master's—in physical education. I did all right. Evidently I was very good on picking professors. I signed up for a very interesting course on Russian history, and the lecturer was excellent. A lot of people knew him pretty well. Usually you wrote a term paper. One day someone said, "Well, let's not write a term paper." And so, okay, let's not write a term paper. A few days later somebody said, "Let's not have a final examination." He said, "Okay, no final examination." So you could just go and listen without the effort of having to stress and strain yourself, and to me that was a very fascinating course. Then, you know, I had to do some research in physical education. Found out what hadn't been done. You'd go through fifty-eleven books and find out it was not there. A lot of that was a waste of time.

SG: *While you were in New York, did you miss Morehead, Kentucky? Did you get homesick or know you wanted to go back to Kentucky?* CLC: No, I was just taking in all I could take in. I don't know how long the summer sessions last, but I went for three summers. I took all my sessions in summer school. I taught up here while I was getting my master's. See, I had one year on my master's and went back and finished it after I started teaching.

SG: *How did you start teaching?* CLC: Well, they decided that they needed a P.E. teacher here in Morehead.

SG: *They hadn't had one before?* CLC: Yes, they had one, but they kind of needed help, and they knew that I had my degree in that, and they asked me if I'd like the job. The president then? I believe it was Long. It was a very small faculty then. When I started, I think Len Miller and Ellis Johnson . . . . I believe they were there. They had good basketball.

SG: *For girls, too?* CLC: No, men. It was just that time they were making all kinds of crazy things. Women's basketball was three courts. You couldn't run from one place to another all over the court. You had three courts. You had certain people in the middle section and certain people on this end and then on that end. I don't know how they ever came up with such a thing. I don't really know why, but I guess they didn't want girls to run that much. Run and stop—like that was hard on their health. They decided—Naismith—they had rules and they decided. They decided about girls' sports, didn't want girls to do too much. I think the primary philosophy was that stopping quickly was hard on women.

SG: *What did they think bearing a child was if that isn't hard on women?* **CLC:** No, it doesn't make sense at all.

SG: *Did you live with your parents then? And what did your mother think then? She didn't want you to even play basketball, and there you are teaching P.E.* **CLC:** Well, she went along with it. Well, I'll tell you, the minute I came back from New York, I knew I was going to med school. Yes, in fact, I was hired that first semester, and I was also taking a course in physics at that time. I needed a course in physics, a prerequisite to go to med school. As a matter of fact, when I got ready to go to med school, that professor had cut my grades and gave me an audit for the course. I took the course not enrolled, so to get credit I paid the fee for the semester.

SG: *What got you truly serious about medical school?* **CLC:** Well, I came back home and thought, "Here you are," and everybody else was doing something, and I wanted to do something, too.

SG: *But you were teaching at the college.* **CLC:** Well, I was already taking physics. Teaching was perfectly satisfactory, but I just didn't feel like I was doing what I was supposed to do. But I loved teaching. Ah, yes, just wasn't what I was supposed to do. I thought a very bad thing when I was teaching. I swore that people should not use teaching as a stepping stone to doing something else. Teaching should be done for teaching itself. I've preached that sermon many times, and here I was. For me it wasn't a stepping stone. It was just a deviation, a detour. And I was kind of scared.

SG: *Scared of what?* **CLC:** Just afraid to really do it. I dreamed, oh, I dreamed about it, like a big amphitheater. You know where it's like the movies. Oh, I don't know, don't know. I'm just a scared person. Well, maybe scared of the challenge. Well, how ignorant I was then. I never thought about money. I never thought, well, where am I going to get the money or how am I going to get the money. That's how ignorant I was. I just wrote checks, and that's what I'd always done.

SG: *So you went to med school. When and where?* **CLC:** I went to med school in the fall of 1943 in Louisville. It was the only one in the state, and that was the logical one. At that time the doctors in Morehead were from Ann Arbor, Cincinnati, and Boston. I talked to Dr. Blair [Don's father] a lot. He told me not to go to med school, not to come back to Morehead, and to do a special thing. Don't do general medicine. So I did everything he told me not to. And he was trying to advise me right, and I would be surprised if he wasn't. He really didn't think that women were the best for medicine. Why did he think that? Because he was a man. **SH:** And he worked real hard. He worked hard. He had done what we did later. **CLC:** Up in the hills, and he'd wade in the mud, and it was a hard life. He thought women were smart enough but that they weren't strong enough. Especially me, his cousin. I was Dan and Etta's daughter. My mother, Etta, was delicate, little, and pretty. Daddy thought she was the prettiest woman there ever was. He said so. Oh, he did it all the time. Reason he married her. He'd say, "She was the prettiest woman that I ever saw."

SG: *Could we back up now and get you and Susie caught up?* I left Susie at fixing her dolls because she's a nurse. Were you taken to doctors and saw nurses or . . . **SH:** Yep, I was always the nurse. Always. I had whooping cough when I was a child. At that time the public health nurse came to the house, and they put a sign on the house, and nobody could come in because at that time whooping cough was a fairly dangerous disease. My sister died of it. Oh, she died of pneumonia, which follows that. She was two years old.

SG: *That must have scared you.* **SH:** You know, no, I felt partially responsible. I was in school, and I brought it home to all of them. But I thought that public health nurse was an awfully nice woman. She had a daughter, she was my same age, and I just thought she was the nicest person. She had on a blue and white nurse outfit, and she had some kind of cap on. But I went to elementary school in a big city. It was a Catholic school. I graduated from elementary, and I went to the Ursuline Academy, an all-girls' school. I took part in everything you were supposed to. I went to football games, and there was a boys' school not too far from there, and we would go down there for sports, and we played volleyball. I wasn't big on sports, but I liked to jump rope. I really like to jump rope. I never had to worry about money, either. I mean, we didn't have the money that Louise's family had, but we were well provided for. My father was in the oil business. My mother never worked outside the home in her life. She was frequently ill. I can remember when my mother died. She didn't even have a social security number.

SG: *In the Catholic school there are so many orders dedicated to nursing. Was that where you were influenced?* **SH:** No, there was no influence there. Where I went into nursing, it was a different congregation. It was Nazareth, and now it's Spaulding—that's Spaulding in Louisville. They have nursing, and that's where I was accepted, so that's where I went. I went straight all year round for three years. Nurse's training is very rigorous. Then, when I graduated from nursing, I went to Clay County. That's in the mountains—East Manchester.

SG: *Why did you go there? Had you ever been in eastern Kentucky?* SH: No. My roommate and I, we went through high school together and nursing together, too. We'd taken our state boards, and we hadn't gotten results on it, and you couldn't work anyplace, but you could work for the state department of health or in your home hospital. So we chose to go with the state department of health, and the hospital in Clay County was run by the state department of health. We went there on our own. We could either have not worked or we could have. Well, there were several things you could do—visiting nurses—but we decided we'd like to go.

SG: *Did you ever waver?* SH: Oh, sure, I quit about a thousand times. I thought, well, I can't do this when I was into chemistry. "What?" I said. "There is no way I can learn this." I mean, science was not my field, and I wondered how I got into it, because I really liked history and things like that a lot better. But there's a lot of nursing history, too. It didn't take long to find there was a lot of hard work to it. It was all hard. I had to study hard. It was mental labor.

SG: *So you left nursing school very optimistic about being a nurse?* SH: Oh, yes. And I was a good student. I wasn't a straight A student, but I studied. I could have studied harder, but I had a hard time with the sciences, I really did, and the math, and there's a lot of that.

SG: *Did you have any specialty in mind?* SH: People back then didn't specialize like they do now, and the funny thing is that Louise—well, I met Louise up in Clay County—and well, I thought there wasn't anything I couldn't do. I was awfully smart at twenty-one. I don't know how I got so smart so quick!

SG: *So you and your friend went off to eastern Kentucky, and you had never been there. Was that a surprise?* SH: Oh, was it ever! First of all, we went by bus, and then we had to wait in Manchester for a long time until there was this one bus that would take you to Oneida, a small area where we were. Well, we finally got there. It took us all day to get from Louisville. I can remember we stopped at Richmond, Kentucky. That was a trip. And then we got on a different line that went to Manchester, and after we got to Manchester, we had to wait for this one bus that went to Oneida. It's about five miles, but we thought we'd never get there—five slow miles. Of course, neither one of us drove.

Back then, people didn't drive. I didn't get my driver's license until I was twenty-five. But when we got there, we did have electricity. We didn't have fresh milk. It was powdered milk, and everything we ate, like meat, was frozen. We'd have to thaw it out the day before. We ate in the cafeteria of the hospital. The hospital was a maternity hospital only, and it had a doctor there who was working. It was a lady doctor from Pennsylvania, and she was going to take her boards, was studying to take her boards in OB-GYN, and that's how Louise happened to come. The bus driver took us right to the hospital. They knew we were coming. They knew these two little new nurses were coming in. They needed help, and it was a very small hospital—twenty-five beds or twenty—but it was a small hospital and everyone knew what everyone else was doing. There was a nurses' house, and then there was a doctor's house right next door, and we were the only two nurses there. Then another one from our class came. **CLC:** Her name was Bessie Hacker in anesthesiology. **SH:** There was one doctor, and eventually there were four nurses. But when we were first there, there was just us. So we had a place to live, a nice house, and we went over to the hospital for our meals, and they had a well-qualified dietitian, and this is where it all amazed me. See, a truck would go to town and bring back frozen foods, meat, everything was frozen, and it just was a way of life I'd never seen before. The people were really nice. There is some coal mining there, but lumber and farming were their main means to make a living. **CLC:** I think mud was the main product. **SH:** Mud! Everywhere there was. It was such a small town. We only took care of maternity.

SG: *Where did everyone else go?* **SH:** Oh, they went to Manchester, five miles down that road. Little kids or whoever got hurt really bad, they went to London.

SG: *What would your days be like?* **SH:** Well, we worked shifts, and with four of us it was pretty good. We alternated shifts of eight hours. Of course, we were in charge, and we had some aides who helped us, and just being out of school we didn't know a great deal of OB. That's one reason we went up there, and you learned *quick* by observation.

SG: *And were you scared?* **SH:** Yes, I was scared. Yeah, I just sat there all the time and, you know, I'd read as labor went along and, well, I sat there with them and I felt like I was comforting, and we didn't have that many in labor at one time. It wasn't like a big hospital. And then you'd have the babies to take care of. But you learned to depend on yourself a lot. Because, in that sort of thing, nature does most of it.

SG: *How many babies do you think you've seen born?* **SH:** Oh, a lot, thousands. Louise has delivered eight thousand, and I've been there for seventy-nine hundred.

SG: *What year did you get to Clay County?* **SH:** The end of 1947.

SG: *And that's where you two met? What was the name of the hospital?* **SH:** Oneida Maternity Hospital.

SG: *So, Dr. Louise, how did you get to this little hospital?* **CLC:** I don't know how I heard about it. I think somebody told me about it. I didn't know. Oh, I was scared to death, too. I drove up there, and I saw that little hospital, and the lady—the doctor there—she seemed so nice, and she helped me get on my feet so I wouldn't be afraid in OB, and she was pretty good in gynecology, so she was going to teach me how to use equipment and so forth. Yes, I graduated in 1946, and I'd done my internship. It was my first job. Yes, I was petrified, too, but I had this security that she was going to help me, she was gonna make me feel free to do this. Her name was Clark. She was from Pennsylvania.

SG: *How old was she at that time?* **SH:** Oh, I thought she was pretty old, probably forty. She went there for the same reason we did. She wanted to get more experience. **CLC:** I think I came there through the public health department to get some more training in delivering babies. **SH:** Because you realized that was going to be one of the things you were going to have to do. **CLC:** You could tell. I'd been with Everett, my cousin, you know, and it seemed like, gosh, every night at three o'clock you had to go out and have a baby. So I felt like I've got to be sure I know what's going on. I knew that eventually I would stay in Morehead. And that's the kind of thing I thought I'd be doing here. Well, I went there and talked with her. I didn't know whether I liked her or not, just scared to death, but I felt it was a good source. So I went to work almost immediately because, I mean, she wanted to study for her boards. But actually what she wanted was to get off, so actually I was to cover while she went. It turned out, well, that gave me a lot of responsibility quick.

SG: *Susie, how long had you been there when Dr. Louise came?* **SH:** Oh, about three months. We were settled in pretty good.

SG: *Do you remember the first time you saw each other?* **SH:** Kind of, I remember. I knew there was a new doctor coming, and then when she came we said, "Gosh, she's pretty nice." My first impression? Well, that doctor was a bigger woman, taller than I am, and Louise was so little. **CLC:** I was five foot two! **SH:** She was *never* that tall! She came over to the nurses. In fact, she spent more time there than in the house next door. **CLC:** Well, I just rattled around over there by myself. And, oh, I went to work immediately. **SH:** Well, I'll tell you what would happen. You know, you didn't call for the doctor until it was time for the baby or getting close to time. We also had clinics in the surrounding areas for prenatal care and, I guess, birth control. **CLC:** And we went to Red Bird, and we went to Manchester and other places. And they had midwives out there, too. **SH:** Yes, but not trained midwives. Most of them we saw at the clinic. But that was Mary Breckinridge and her nurses on horseback. But they were not too far from there, and they ran a clinic at Red Bird. **CLC:** They ran that? Well, what were we doing there?

SG: *Did you find you could work together with ease right away? Or how did it develop that you could work together so well?* **SH:** I don't know what actually did. We all worked well together up there. I thought we did. I couldn't see that we worked better together than anyone else. Louise was actually trying to get *anybody* that would come to Morehead. I was the only one that would come to Morehead, and I decided to stay a year here. I didn't care what happened. **CLC:** I had to have somebody that was willing to stay in a place like that.

SG: *How long were you both in Clay County?* **SH:** I was there for six months, and Louise was there for three months.

SG: *Did you learn a lot?* **CLC:** Yes, I learned to be scared to death. Oh, I got better.

SG: *Do you think scared is the right word? Dealing with other people's lives, you've got to be anxious in a way. No matter what you do, don't you have to wonder if you are good enough?* **CLC:** No, I think actually I was pretty satisfied with what we did up there. Like this one lady we were telling you about . . . **SH:** The lady with the retained placenta, the afterbirth. The nurses were sending her down from Red Bird. So Louise got out her book and read everything and, oh, we had that delivery room set up when she got there. I gave the anesthesia, and Louise was going to deliver this placenta. She knew exactly what to do. Before I even gave a drop of anesthesia, she put her hand on her abdomen and out came the placenta, just like that. Magic. **CLC:** Magic! And here we were all scared to death. Maybe the rough road jogged it loose.

SG: *You say you were scared, but then you said that nature pretty well does it. Is delivering babies always a thrill, a miracle?* **CLC:** In the end it is. I mean, it is a great satisfaction. And when you look at 'em, they're not doin' a thing. Then they jerk up and start that a-cryin'. Oh, why, I swear, there's nothin' like it.

SG: *And you don't get bored with it?* **CLC:** No.

SG: *When was the last baby?* **SH:** It was ten years ago. I think December 6. It was eleven years this December. **CLC:** But, oh, Lord, those little old breeches.

SG: *Pants?* **CLC:** Oh, they're fun. **SH:** No, breeches. **CLC:** You know, they come bottom first. And you have to reach in and turn . . . **SH:** You know, people aren't taught how to do it anymore. We were taught how to do it for breech, but as time went on, people stopped doing that when they had C-sections.

SG: *Is that because it's easier on the doctor?* **SH:** It's easier on all concerned. It just usually takes assistance. **CLC:** And you have to wait. You have to wait, that's it. And you think, oh, laws, that's it, but you can't get a-hold of it. **SH:** You have to wait until it comes down far enough. **CLC:** Then you just fit in there and slide it out. You watch it and then you get a-hold of it and you slide it back in and slide it around. It's there doing nothing, and then you slide it around and the butt just raises up and you can see it, then get a-hold of it, and you just turn it around. Sometimes a foot is down or two feet are down. Sometimes it's a flat butt, but if it's just a flat butt you usually have to go up in there and turn a leg down and pull it down and hold it and go up and get the other one and pull it down and then you pull the two of 'em out together. Then you twist it around to the shoulders and then get your hand in there and you pull down, and you pull down that arm and hook a finger in the mouth and then the other arm, and then twist, and then there it is! Oh, that's really fun!

SG: *What do you feel when you're the ones really watching what really happens? Is it sort of a thrill, or relief, or what do you feel?* **CLC:** Oh, laws, it's a great thrill. Oh, yes, it's just like you hit a good clear high note. **SH:** It's not always the same, but it's most always pleasant, most always.

SG: *What about those tong things you loaned for the play? Was that illegal?* **CLC:** No, no. We borrowed those. They're not illegal. They're used a lot. But if you had an epidural, all babies were delivered by forceps. **SH:** Oh, you can't tell it if you don't know it. **CLC:** It's very simple.

SG: *Did you do many deliveries in people's homes?* **SH:** We did from 1948 until 1957.

SG: *Oh, almost ten years. You were talking about slogging through the mud?* **SH:** Seems it was mud. Our roads weren't as good as they are now. Then we had a man from Elliott County Road Commission, and he built a lot of good roads around here.

SG: *I don't really want to wear you out, but could we just get you to Morehead today? How did that come about?* **CLC:** Oh, I'd already decided that's where I was going to start in January. I was going to be a general practitioner. Well, my daddy had a building that I could use, and it was upstairs over the pool room. That building is still there. Upstairs is not anything now. Downstairs is a fraternity house, and next to it is a barbershop, and on the opposite side is a restaurant.

SG: *So you knew you were coming back to Morehead. Did you have to buy a lot of equipment to get started?* SH: We picked it out up there [Clay County]. We got an X-ray machine and . . . CLC: And ammonium chloride tablets . . . SH: And, oh, yes, ammonium chloride, which is a diuretic. Why, we got enough to last a hundred years. We didn't know any better. Used to be used as a diuretic. It's not used anymore, I don't believe. This was a pill. You used to give it to people with heart failure. Now you give them things like Lasix. No, we didn't have catalogs, but the drug people came and talked to us. In those three months we did it all. I guess by Christmas time I knew I was coming. Well, I'd been through Morehead on my way to Charleston once. That was it. And I knew that there was a school here and I was going to take classes.

SG: *To up your degree?* SH: Oh, no. I was going to take art appreciation, things like that. CLC: She was very good in art. Did a lot of drawing and things of that sort. SH: Well, I wasn't sure I would fit in this situation, but it was a lot better than Oneida, let me tell you. They had a school there in Oneida, and I went to high school basketball games. That was about it. Dances and things. That was our entertainment. Better than Clay County, let me tell you. Actually, I came to Morehead before Louise did. Louise was in New York when I got here. And this friend of hers from China was here, Dr. Huai Mei Chen. They'd gone to school together, and she was going back to China. Anyway, Louise was up there in New York. So Louise's mother and I started to get the office ready. We painted. Oh, yes, when I first came, there was snow. There was snow everywhere, and I got off the train and Jane and Boone met me, Louise's brother and his wife, and I went up to their house. And Jane had been on a sleigh ride the night before, and their house was kind of a mess, and there was ketchup on the fireplace and I thought, "Oh, my Lord, what have I gotten into?" But she had a good meal, and her house—well, she hadn't cleaned up around the fireplace yet. I guess it was about a week before Louise got back from New York. The first day when Granny and I went down there to clean, oh, we cleaned and cleaned and scrubbed and painted. Granny was a good scrubber! And Louise and I stayed at Louise's mother's house at first, and we went to that office early, I remember. And I thought we never would have a next meal. Finally, at about three or four o'clock in the afternoon Louise's sister Patty, who was home from somewhere, brought us some tomato soup. **CLC:** Susie couldn't get over not having three meals a day. **SH:** Yeah, where I came from you ate three meals a day and everybody sat down at a table. **CLC:** Nothing was like that at our house.

SG: *This is that big white house on Wilson Avenue? 326 Wilson Avenue? That must be a big house.* **CLC:** There was the front room, and the main room, and my room, the blue room, and the front room, and the downstairs nursery. **SH:** And then, when we started that practice, it didn't take long until we were real busy. The first week or two we didn't do much, but every day it would get more.

SG: *Only a week or two? I've heard some doctors say it can be six months or a year.* **SH:** But we got there every day, every day, and we were there until closing time, even when we weren't doing anything. We worked every day, six days with two afternoons off. And then for a while we had night office hours, but that didn't work out. People didn't come, so we quit that.

SG: *Did you have someone to work in your office?* **SH:** In the very beginning we didn't. Jane did it for a while and then Merle, her sister-in-law.

SG: *Do you remember your first patient?* **SH:** Oh, it was Mildred Bradley. First one in the door. She and her husband ran a florist's shop. Neither one of us knew her, but Louise knew her husband, but she was from California and she thought she was pregnant—and she was. So she was our first patient.

Eldon "Tick" Evans
February 8, 1993

Eldon "Tick" Evans was interviewed for several reasons other than because he was a friend of Dr. Louise. Evans was mayor of Morehead at the time Louise and Susie began their campaign to solicit funds and support for building a hospital. His story of how Louise first approached him to solicit donations is one of the most charming, and the most telling about Louise's determination. Evans was also the elder brother of Louise's close childhood friend Sidney Evans, and it was at the Evans family home where most of their childhood games were played. (Mr. Evans died October 26, 1994.)

You know, I won't tell you something unless I know. Now, we all played together. Louise lived on Main Street, and she and Lucille and Boone and Sis played together. I had two sisters and a brother [Sidney, Gladys, and Drew]. My brother got killed. When we were little, there was four of us. But Gladys, she was just a little thing—she's seven years younger than me. She was just a little thing and, of course, I was the oldest and maybe ten or eleven years old, and we made candy at Louise's home. And we'd make candy at our home. We'd make candy because in those days there really wasn't much to do for entertainment. There was just the entertainment that you made yourself.

Back then, Louise was very active. She was athletic. She would play football with the boys. Oh, they were little tykes. They didn't care. They didn't pay any attention. You know what I mean. And as I told you, she and Sis [Sidney]—they'd go up a door like this, hand-walking up a doorjamb. They'd get on this door and they'd up, up, up the sides. My sister Sidney was athletic, too. Oh, yes. But Louise was very much more athletic. And she rode our pony. The pony's name was Betsy Ross. We didn't have the pony there at the house; we had a farm.

Now, Louise and them, they all went to high school together and grade school, too. We were together, but I wasn't in the same grade. In the same school building. She and her older sister Lucille both. I was in Lucille's grade. Louise graduated from high school, and she went from there to Ohio State in physical education. And she graduated and came back and taught physical education here at MSU. And then I don't remember but it seems to me that while I was in the service, Louise went to medical school. I don't know, but I think she went to Louisville. About that time they were passing laws that required so much service. The government paid you. The government paid so much of your expense, but you had to obligate yourself to do so much community work. Is that the correct way? Then she graduated from there and, of course, went down into southeastern Kentucky, down into Clay County, through there.

Then she came back here and she put an office up over those poolrooms. The building is still there. And, if I'm not mistaken, she had an X-ray machine in there. And the funniest thing I remember, I looked up one day and saw Louise and Susie with their heads sticking out the window. I said, "What you up there doin'?" She said, "We're looking for patients." She said, "Do you think we'll make it?" I said, "Well, I think you will." Now, that was their beginning of practice here in Morehead. And, of course, you know the history from there on. Patients just multiplied.

And now, on the hospital. This is my recollection. Louise came here to the house one Saturday afternoon. I was taking a shower. My family was in Florida. They were coming back from Florida, and they'd had car trouble, and they were in Knoxville, Tennessee. I was taking a shower, getting dressed. So there's somebody at the door. I didn't want to answer the door, shorts and all, so Louise just opened the door and came in! She and Susie. And I was in that room there, dressing. And there's a step just before that room. She sat down on the step while I was dressing and told me about a hospital. This is true. And I said, "Have you talked to my friend John Palmer?" He lived here next door to me. He was a sales manager for Lee Clay products. He was a personal friend of mine. We went to church together. So I said, "Did you talk to my friend?" She said, "Yeah, I talked to John," she says, "and I want to put a hospital here in Morehead." She said, "I've talked to the Methodists and I've talked to the Baptists and all of them to try to get them to run it, and they won't run it. But I can get the Catholics to do it." So now this is the part you're looking for, isn't it? So she started asking people in town for both money and interest. Now, I've forgotten how much money she wanted. And so she started getting pledges for so much over a period of three years.

Oh, well, they all wished they had a hospital here in town, but no one wished it hard enough to want to work on it. I don't know if there was even much talk about it. They wanted a hospital here, but didn't do anything about it until she took over. That's my opinion.

Well, so there I was trying to get dressed and she was telling me about this hospital. So I said, "I haven't got the time to talk to you." I said, "I've got to go and get some money." But she stayed there until I got dressed and ready to leave and I went out and got in the car. She got in the car with me! We drove down to the Eagle's Nest Restaurant to get a check cashed. And I took off to Knoxville. And so that interest, she got the interest started. Louise was the founder of that hospital. That's my opinion.

Now, she ran into some opposition. So, anyway, we started having meetings, dinners and we had Monsignor something . . . can't recall the name, but he helped Louise. So eventually we had—I've forgotten, but it wasn't so awfully much money in terms of today, but back then, well, a dollar was a little bigger then. So it just kept on until they finally gave the go ahead decision. Then, after we had the hospital, we didn't have anything for the clinic, so then she had to sell them on the idea of a clinic. That was a building over on the other side for the doctors.

Now, maybe I'm getting ahead of my story. She talked to the board of directors. . . . Wait a minute, they started to get a hospital. They organized a foundation, the Northeastern Kentucky Hospital Foundation, that raised the money. And that Northeastern Kentucky Foundation . . . there were twelve on the board. I wasn't on it originally, until after about a year.

So we got the hospital and then we had to go out and get some doctors. We got Dr. Warren Proudfoot. Then we raised enough money, not for the hospital, but for this foundation itself to build a small clinic. Not the Morehead Clinic. Another little clinic. We dissolved that and gave it to the hospital. Anyway, we, the board of directors at that time, we guaranteed these doctors' salaries. And the directors—Louise, she promoted this—she's promoting all of this, you see what I'm saying? She was the wheel that made this thing go. So the board of directors signed a note for, I believe, $2,500 to guarantee these doctors' salaries. So then we deposited this money. So they opened up.

See this? Here's a pen and pencil set passed out for being on the board of directors. I was the treasurer. It says "1963. In appreciation. Eldon T. Evans. Northeast Kentucky Hospital Foundation. 1963-1988. Twenty-five years of caring." And it was established, and you know what the first addition was? They got that first addition, then Louise just kept trying. She just kept trying. And, of course, then they got this second addition. Now she has helped with getting this third addition. She was involved with it.

Now, with the hospital foundation she is the president or was the president. She was the president of the remainder of the foundation and the foundation has, oh, about $25,000. Now, this money—well, when the doctors got so they could take it in, they said we don't want that. So they moved out. So we took all that and converted it into money. We gave some money to the hospital foundation and to some health organization. That money has never been used except for the organization. I think we've got $25,000 some. Now, we have been giving the income from this money to the school as a scholarship in honor of Louise. Now, I'm just jumping from here to there. So at the last meeting, we're not going to have any more board of directors. We're just going to let it die off. The last director that there is is going to be the treasurer. And then the money that we have left, he will turn it over to the school as a Louise Caudill Scholarship. We've already got the scholarship up there, you see, for nursing students.

I was mayor from 1960, while the hospital was going on. Well, the interstate was being built. The school was big, and I was interested in the water and sewer and the widening of the creek. Well, the sewer wasn't big enough. With the hospital being built and the school growing, wasn't that something that had to be thought about? Yes, it all goes together. No, I didn't run for mayor again. I didn't want to go the second go around. But I had to see this thing through. That was to take these little narrow creeks and make them much wider. That was for flood control. Then there is the sewer plant downtown. Now they've got a good waterworks, a good sewer plant.

You see, my cattle over on the farm, if I want to let them, they drink the same water that you drink. You see, we were a rural community—you follow what I'm saying—when I grew up. No electric. We were just rural. The school came here in 1922-23. My brother and I, they sent us in 1923 and we didn't like it very much. I was thirteen and my brother was eleven. We had indoor plumbing, but most of the houses didn't. There were outhouses, with two and three holes, even in the town, and little boys would go around and push them over. Oh, yes, I did, too! Little kids weren't supposed to, but they did.

We played, too. There at our home we had croquet grounds. And on the back, on the side next to Perry Ave., there was a great football boundary. That's where Louise and them played, the little kids, you know. And on the other side was the garden. Now that's where we stole the corn roasting ears. Oh, we did everything! We stole roasting ears of corn. My mother used a paddle or a switch, but my daddy, he didn't. He wasn't home much. And Mother, oh, she fussed at us for stealing the corn.

Now, Daddy, he was a good gardener. He loved it, and he made me and my brother love it, too. He was really in the lumber business and he was away, oh, half of the time. And when he'd come in, well, me and my brother would be sitting here waiting for him. Then we'd go swimming over here in this creek. Now, honey, back then that creek was just so clear you could see a dime. Pure. And there wasn't any contamination, and we'd wait until he came in. He'd have his suitcase and walk up through the garden, look, and say, "Well, boys, you've done a pretty good job" or "Boys, you haven't done a pretty good job." If we hadn't done a pretty good job, we'd have to go back and do it over again. Anyway, the kids would go swimming in that creek.

Oh, yes, Betsy Ross. Now, that gang that put the pony in the attic, I forgot to tell you about that. Well, I wasn't one of them. My brother, Drew Jr., he'd do anything. And he got the pony and Louise and Sis and, I don't know, there was a big bunch of them. They got the pony, and they brought it right through the front door. Hardwood floors. They took it on up the stairs. The stairs were carpeted. They took it up there and then they took it on up to the attic stairs. They weren't much over two and a half feet and up a curve. Look over at that picture of the house. See that dormer up on the third floor? That's where they had the pony's head sticking out. Yes, well, somebody went down the street and got my mother and they said, "Mrs. Evans, they've got the pony's head sticking out that attic window." She said, "Lord, have mercy. What will those young-uns do next?" She came up straight and made them bring it back down. Well, how they got it up there—I've heard different stories. I think they all got in there and maybe some of them pushed a little bit.

Well, that pony was easy to get along with. It was a pet. Only forty inches high. The pony, oh, I told you, we had this place up at the branch— and we'd go up and get that pony. Some of them would, and they wanted to ride it. They'd bring it down and put it out there in the yard. We had a hedge around that yard and they'd play with the pony. And the pony would get tired of it and it would shake its bridle down and shove off and take off right up through town and go for the barn. Just to get away from those kids.

Now, Louise is still my doctor. People, not only here but all around, they come to her rather than just any doctor. Women come to her, but a lot of men come to her, too. She used to make house calls, and that's about unheard of now.

She's been very supportive of the Christian Church, and I don't even know what other charities she helps. For many years, people thought that she and Bob Bishop would get married. Well, Bob's father passed away the night he graduated from high school. So he took the drugstore over . . . medicine sales. They used to go to New York plays together. Bob was fixing to have his eyes worked on. And he got a second opinion and if "Doc" okayed it, it was all right.

I'll tell you a little story. Now, this was the occasion, but a nurse at the hospital told me that Bob went in out there to the emergency room and they said, "Who's your doctor?" And he said, "Louise. Louise Caudill."

And they said, "We can't get Louise. She's out. She's at a hospital board meeting." And they told her, and she left that hospital board meeting to take care of Bob. They're really good friends.

Now, you see all that medicine over there. I'm getting ready to leave for a few days, but I call down there for more and if she wants me to she'll say, "Come down," and if not she'll say, "I'll call the drugstore and have them send you some medicine." I came home from Florida with gout. I could hardly walk. So I got down there and said, "Oh, I want to see Louise." I had an old pair of house slippers on. She said, "Boy, I know you're sick if you come down here looking like that!"

Well, she's a very kind and caring person. Does that sound right? She's genuine. That's a good word. I have to be careful with you school teachers!

Dr. Claire Louise Caudill and Susie Halbleib
January 13, 1993

On our third morning together we began to talk about how the town got together and really got serious about building a good hospital. A great many names are mentioned, of people who were crucial in the money raising and community organization. Many of the people who first worked for the hospital are still here, and a few of the backers, including MSU president Adron Doran, still return. Dr. Warren Proudfoot, who become a beloved physician here, is gone now, but his son is in practice. Dr. Richard Carpenter has left, but Dr. George Barber remains on the hospital staff. Now, for most residents, it is hard to remember the town without the hospital.

SG: *Let me ask you two things first. One is, somebody told me to ask you about taking a horse upstairs.* **CLC**: Oh, we were kids. Sidney Evans, this girl I played with most of the time, they had a pony. And that pony, oh, it had a heck of a life. We did everything to that pony. The Evanses had the best house in town. It's terrible they tore it down and built that bank [Morehead National Bank on Main Street]. **SH**: That's recently, within the last ten years. **CLC**: Oh, it had all inlaid floors. Had gorgeous big mantels. And we took that pony upstairs, all the way to the third floor of that house, and we tried to make it stick its head out the window up there, and that thing wouldn't do it. Well, we took it back down to the second floor and tried to get it in the bathtub, and it wouldn't do that, either. We took that little pony about every place—there were five of us and we rode it at the same time. It was just about that long.
SG: *Also, would you mind if I talked to other people about you?* **CLC**: Oh, you can talk to anybody. It might be better than talking to me.
SG: *Why?* **CLC**: Oh, I don't tell things very well.
SG: *I was wondering if today we could talk about the hospital. How it started, where the idea came from, all of that. You know, we get impossible ideas of how we'd like places to have things. How does it start?* **CLC**: I don't know where it started really. I mean, as you worked you knew you were not efficient. You couldn't do what you wanted to do. And you couldn't take just your hands and go about practicing medicine and doing much good and, I mean, that's just the way life was at

that time. We talked a lot. Susie and I talked an awful lot about medicine and about what we wanted to do. You know, we ended up—well, for six or seven years people would yell up at us in the middle of the night to get up and go someplace. See, people knew where our bedrooms were, and they'd yell upstairs for us to come. **SH:** Throw rocks at the windows. **CLC:** Oh, they came once and yelled up at us for a baby to be delivered, and I went back to sleep, and Susie came and whispered to me, "Get up, Louise. We've got to go!" And I rolled over and said, "Oh, no, we don't. They called just now and said they were at the Midland Trail Garage on their way to Lexington." But I dreamed that. I mean, you couldn't just live like that. **SH:** People usually came to the door and knocked hard or called on the telephone. **CLC:** But how the hospital got started. The notion for a hospital. I'd say there was a lot of talk around here, and people asked me about maybe starting a hospital. Well, Susie and I talked it over, and we didn't think there was any way we could do that. You know, they didn't know exactly what they were talking about because there is more to it. And then there was a fella that came through here from the state department of health and I can't remember his name. **SH:** C.C. Howard. **CLC:** And he came down to the office one day. Oh, he'd made a call someplace here, but he came to our office. Then we had our office where we are now, and we had babies there and so forth. And he said, "Well, why don't you start a hospital?" And we gave him our reason—we really thought it was true—we didn't want one unless it was a good one. We'd seen a lot of them. And we'd seen hospitals where they did everything whether they needed it or not. So we didn't want that. That's what I told him, and he knew the kind of hospital I was talking about. He'd seen 'em, too. He said, "Well, if you want one and you want to work hard enough, you can get it." So I was stubborn and that aggravated me. Oh, I guess we talked every night for a month, didn't we? About can you do that? Can you have a good one, and if you can, how can you? So we went over and around and—you had to have a facility, of course. You had to have people to run it. You had to have physicians, and you had to have specialty groups, and you had to have the community who wanted it. And you had to have the money. So we couldn't do anything but find out if the community wanted it and if we could get some money. Out of that we decided what was our first issue. So any day we closed the office in daylight, we'd just go house to house or business to business. **SH:** And we went to people who had money.
SG: *Did you start out with a list?* **CLC:** No, just what was in our head. **SH:** See, it used to be we knew everybody in town and we knew ev-

erybody at the university. **CLC:** I think we started in August of 1960. **SH:** At the office we started in 1957, but I think we started this project, the door knocking, in the summer. **CLC:** We just did that from August until October, wasn't it? Somewhere about like that, and we did pretty good. We didn't ask people to give us money. No, we told 'em what we wanted to do, and I think we had pledges of about $87,000. **SH:** Oh, we had an awful lot of people who said they would give. **CLC:** Yes, but you didn't write anything down.

SG: *Was the interest in building a hospital one hundred percent?* **CLC:** No, but the interest was high. **SH:** It was high, and the people we asked mostly were interested because that's who we went to—people we felt would care the most and wanted to give. We thought money was the big part of it then, and it still is, but it's not near as big a part as all the rest of it.

SG: *You said you wanted a good hospital. What was bad about the ones that you wanted to avoid?* **CLC:** We didn't want surgery that didn't need to be done. I'd seen that.

SG: *You mean surgery just to make money, or careless, sloppy surgery?* **CLC:** Well, you can just make your own judgment. We felt that they were just doing it to satisfy people and also to make money. You know, a lot of people like to be cut on. I really believe that. You see, that's what we mean by unnecessary surgery. **SH:** And poor medicine. **CLC:** We wanted people who were qualified and who knew what they were doing. And just a practitioner *can't* do everything. They just are not qualified to do everything. You can't read your own X rays and cut out your specimen or do that whole job. We tried it, and some of it didn't work that good. Oh, we tried doing some GI X rays and kidney X rays . . . **SH:** And by the time we did it all—and I mean it's a big procedure— you know, giving them barium and all and then send them off to be read, well, it's more trouble than it's worth. It's much easier to have the patient go to Lexington and get it done and get a report in writing. And we were concerned about a patient, and we just weren't very good at that procedure.

SG: *Were people expecting you to—well, that a doctor knows everything?* **CLC:** No, they didn't. But I did—for myself, I guess more so. I just hated—well, you knew there was more that you could do to make that diagnosis and you didn't feel that you could slip it over.

SG: *Had you seen people who did that kind of work and that's why you thought it was a bad hospital?* **CLC:** Well, I hate to say that people were bad . . . **SH:** They probably didn't mean to be. But there are and there were . . . **CLC:** Well, they weren't trained. **SH:** And there weren't as many laws then. Oh, there wasn't so much government interference then. You know, you could operate your own little hospital. And they did a lot of good, but they were not very good hospitals in some cases. I can't mention where they were, and never in Morehead.

SG: *Now there is an emergency ward here. What would have been the equivalent then of going to an emergency ward? If you got cut or broke your leg or had a serious accident, would you go to Lexington?* CLC: Oh, many times we'd fix it. We'd fix broken arms.

SG: *So first you went out to see if the community wanted a hospital.* CLC: Yes, and at the time they seemed to be interested. And then when they were interested you had to see, well, what you had to do next. And then you wanted somebody to run it. We had friends in most of the churches. Susie was Catholic, and I was Christian [Christian Church on Main Street]. Some of the people we'd asked were Methodists and Baptists and they ran hospitals, so we asked them what to do, and everybody said they didn't have any money—with the exception of the Catholic Church. And they didn't exactly say that they had a lot of money, but they said that they thought they could help some. SH: They said they'd look into it. CLC: Anyhow, it wasn't very long until they came and said they *were* interested.

SG: *But, Susie, you were saying how very small the Catholic population here was.* SH: It was tiny. Like a dozen. I mean, well, there were a few students, too, from the university, but they weren't permanent as far as you could count them. Mass was, well, there was a garage right where the church is now. There was a house there, and it had a garage, and mass was there. A priest came over from Maysville on Sundays.

SG: *So even though there were only a dozen or so Catholics here, it was the Catholic Church that was interested. Interested in running it or in supporting it?* SH: Running it was what we were looking for then. CLC: Administration. The Sisters of Notre Dame had this hospital in Lynch in a coal mining area. They had closed that down, or they were in the process of closing it down. And they had a few nurses, not very many, and I think it was in a transition period for them. Monsignor Towell was the leader really. He was in charge of health at that phase— *at the community.* And he was friendly with the Sisters of Notre Dame. So he came to the office after, oh, who was the priest up there then? Well, anyway, he's the one who sent Monsignor Towell to us. And of all the things—well, I think I tell this right, but I could get something a little bit crooked because—Susie, you might have to correct me some-place along the line. So he came by one morning about ten o'clock on his way to Frankfort. And we had had two sets of twins and a single-

ton [one baby] that night, and we had just had another one and someone in the labor room. So we had babies lined up. We kept them there,
in our office on Main Street, usually about five or six hours, just until
they woke up. So there were five babies all lined up. And he came in
and kind of went pale. He thought surely we must need a hospital. **SH:**
It was impressive, all those babies lined up and we didn't know he was
coming. **CLC:** No, we didn't know he was coming that day. Well, we
never did have that many before. **SH:** No, not all at one time. **CLC:**
But he just walked right in in the middle of it. So he was very much
interested in helping us. I think he was going to do something about
the Hill-Burton government grants that day.

SG: *Do you recall what he said when he came in?* CLC: Just something
like that—"It looks like you need a hospital."

SG: *Did you have little beds or bassinets for these babies?* **SH:** Oh no,
we just had one bassinet. We just lined them up along the couch. We
had five babies on that couch. The mothers were wanting to rest, and
we had them there across the hall. **CLC:** Oh, we had one on the X-
ray table. **SH:** Yes, on the X-ray table, a hard table. One was in the
treatment room. **CLC:** And two mothers were in beds.

SG: *And were there other people in the office, coming in for anything else?*
CLC: Oh, yes, the office was just going on. The babies were on the
couch in the back. Nobody saw them.

SG: *Did you always keep them a short time?* CLC: Oh, yes, unless there
was bleeding or something. About just like they do now. So he saw all
this and said, "You need a hospital," and he told us to write to him in a
letter about what we did every day. *I found that letter. I think I can find
it again.* So I wrote down everything we did *in a day* and sent it off to
him.

Monsignor Chas. A. Towell
St. Agnes Church, Covington, Kentucky
Dear Monsignor:

Enclosed you will find an itemized account of a day's office
procedure as of October 3rd, 1960, along with a brief description
of Morehead and surrounding community in relationship to our
need for hospital facilities.

We did not do a complete week of office procedure because
of lack of time, and we also decided it would take a considerable
amount of your valuable time to read it. This day, however, is quite
typical of most every day.

We wish to express our sincere thanks and gratitude to you

for your excellent cooperation and interest in securing Sisters for the hospital. We understand that the Notre Dame order is "tops."

We hope that the enclosed material is in accordance with your request. If you should need additional information, please contact me and we will be glad to furnish it.

Respectfully,
C. Louise Caudill, M.D.

List of Patients, Monday, October 3.

3 A.M. Patient admitted in labor.
7:30 Breakfast.
9 A.M. Started seeing patients in the office.
    1. Routine prenatal checkup.
    2. 42-year-old woman—post lung resection—cardiac decomp.
9:30 A.M. Admitted a woman in labor.
    3. 15-year-old girl—too fat.
    4. 55-year-old woman—hypertension.
    5. 6-week-old infant with pneumonia.
    6. 30-year-old man with gastritis and emotional problems.
    7. 75-year-old woman with infected finger.
    8. 40-year-old woman—vaginitis.
11:30 A.M. Delivered (3 a.m.) patient of a pretty little girl.
    9. 45-year-old woman—complete physical.
    10. 38-year-old man—upper respiratory infection.
    11. 36-year-old woman—vaginitis.
    12. 6-year-old well-baby checkup.
    13. 60-year-old woman—routine exam.
    14. 4-year-old child—upper respiratory infection.
    15. 34-year-old man—lacerations on three fingers—suturing.
    16. 30-year-old woman—routine pelvic and cauterization.
2 P.M. Delivered (9:30 a.m.) labor admission, a handsome crying boy.
    17. 70-year-old lady—hypertension.
    18. 37-year-old man—prostatitis.
    19. 18-year-old college student—broken finger.
    20. 19-year-old boy, college student—right knee injured, football. Fluid aspirated. TBA injected.
    21. 4-week-old baby—feeding problems.
    22. 6-month-old baby—diarrhea and vomiting.
    23. 16-year-old girl—upper respiratory infection.
    24. 3-year-old boy—upper respiratory infection.
    25. 75-year-old woman—cystitis.

26. 26-year-old woman—prenatal checkup.
27. Routine prenatal.
28. 60-year-old woman—diabetes.
29. 55-year-old woman—car wreck four days ago, sutures removed.
30. 28-year-old man—metal burn on foot.
31. 59-year-old man—fear cancer of lung.
32. 11-year-old boy—fight at school, chin laceration, rock.
33. 17-year-old girl—upper respiratory infection.
34. 20-year-old girl, college student—lymph nodes, bad tooth.
35. 13-year-old boy—tonsillitis.
36. 19-year-old girl—pregnant, mass in breast. Referred to Lexington—sutures removed.

Also, fifteen immunizations, three allergy shots, four dressings changed, one house call. Finished at office at 7:55 and then made house calls.

We wish to express our sincere thanks and gratitude to you for your excellent cooperation and interest in securing Sisters for the hospital.

Respectfully,

C. Louise Caudill

Well, so then we had somebody [the Sisters of Notre Dame] to run it, but we didn't have anything for them to run. So we had to find some doctors. Oh, lord, I had no more idea than a jackrabbit. Well, I used to go over to Lexington to a clinic program. They had some pretty good medical programs, like continuing education. So I went down there, and there I was sitting right next to Dr. Segnitz. Dr. Richard Segnitz was a pediatric surgeon in Lexington. Think he was supposed to be the only one in the state. He was really just the kindest thing you ever knew. And I talked to him all the time, and so I told him what we were trying to do. I told him we sort of needed someone to find doctors for us and get the medicine lined up. And we talked, and when the meeting was over he started over across the road there as fast as he could go, and I started out after him as fast as I could go, and told him I'd like to talk with him some more.

I said we needed somebody really right away. He said, "Well, I might be able to find you somebody." I said, "That would be great. Who would that be?"

And he said, "Well, maybe I would. Maybe I'd be interested." He said, "I know everybody over at the University of Kentucky."

See, the university was just starting a medical school. He knew all the new doctors that were coming in. He worked with them. So he became my buddy from then on. He'd come to Morehead. Brought his children along, and they went fishing one time. Anytime they'd go through, they'd stop. And we went down there [to Lexington] and talked with him, and we knew almost all the new doctors down there then. The main one, the dean of the med school, was Dr. William Willard. He was a good-un. He wanted to do at the university what we wanted to do. Modern medicine, you know, continuing care, and having people who knew from the base of medicine all the way up, tertiary care. And he wanted at the university to have the students learn this common primary type care of medicine as well as the tertiary care. So his philosophy was to send students out to Morehead, or out to someplace so they could see what actually went on . . . when you didn't have all the equipment and so on. I mean, it was great reasoning, I thought, on his part. At least as far as we were concerned.

SG: *And he was the dean of the UK medical school?* CLC: And he became president of the Appalachian Regional Hospital Association. He's done a whole lot. He just resigned, I think, last year. And Bob Johnson came here real often. He wrote grants and helped us get everything started and helped get doctors. And our doctors would go over and work on the staff at the university for, say, a day, a week, or so and do surgical rounds or cardiology rounds. So we had a kind of specialized medicine. One thing that happens, which to me is always the thing that makes you go downhill, as soon as you went back to the country to practice, you lost contact. So you had to have some way of having continuing education. You can go out and take a course or something like that, but you do need something to keep you wound up all the time. So they would make that connection. They would let you in down there and you could get in on whatever was going on. And Dr. Ed Pellegrino, when he came over, he was very much interested in that. He's the one who tried to help us get a little more of the attitude of Hunterdon. You don't know what that is. It's a hospital out in the country that has tried to do everything. They tried to do all the specialties. Everything. And that was a part of the hospital. Outside was the family practitioner. Nobody could get in that hospital except through the family practitioner to the specialist.

SG: *The idea of a cooperative?* CLC: Well, the idea being to spread medicine broader. If you needed a specialist, you'd get a specialist. You didn't waste the specialist's time. Now, we were trying to do something similar. SH: Hunterdon is in Flemington, New Jersey. CLC: I think it's named after a fella. Who was that real rich fella? Anyway, Sister Mary Edwin, Dr. Segnitz, and Susie and I went up there. So it was set up to facilitate—to use your manpower where manpower was needed. **SH:** People also stayed in the hospital, and the doctors' office was right there. That is the surgeon and the radiologist, etc.

SG: *How did you hear about this hospital?* **CLC:** Dr. Pellegrino. He was from the university, and he was the head of medicine. **SH:** He started that out there, that concept. And we liked the idea. Well, that's what we started . . .

SG: *You mean you couldn't make it work?* **CLC:** No, they had another little rule or two. You see, there all the specialists made the same amount of money.

SG: *Maybe a little too socialist? This is the salary, and this is all you can earn.* **CLC:** Yes, and that's what everybody felt—oh, that's socialist. But there's lotsa ways that doesn't work. Because we heard it up there, so we weren't "plumb pushed" by the salary angle. And it all had to be the same. It wasn't a perfect setup. **SH:** Actually, the surgeons did make more in the beginning. **CLC:** Well, in the first year they did, but before the year was out they changed. **SH:** They were guaranteed salaries. **CLC:** See, we formed a group called the Northeastern Kentucky Hospital Foundation. And all we did was to pick out people in town that were really interested in trying to get something going—like Adron Doran—he was a big guy. The thing that's wrong right now is that we don't have the newspaper. But then we had "Snooks" Crutcher, and he was the editor of the newspaper. W.C. Crutcher, he was the owner and the editor. **SH:** He was fantastic. **CLC:** But, I mean, if he wanted something done, he'd put it all over the paper. You didn't have any problem spreading the news. And then Dr. Doran told the teachers up at the university that they had better want a hospital here, too, and he got a little extra help, I think. And Doran was on the board, and Snooks was on the board, and there was one place that was very important in Morehead and that was the Eagle's Nest. You ever heard of the Eagle's Nest? **SH:** It was a restaurant. **CLC:** It's not there anymore. It was a restaurant, and it was pretty well known in its time. If anybody went through Morehead, that was the place you stopped. And they had the best biscuits and the best pies and the best country ham. It was really good. And Chin Clayton ran that. And everybody knew Chin, and he knew everybody, so he was on the board. **SH:** It used to be down on West Main Street, about where Arby's is now. **CLC:** It was right across from the Citizens' Bank. Right, it was sort of the town hub. All the problems of the town were solved there. Come ten o'clock, "the group" would meet. **SH:** For coffee and pie. The men in the morning and the women went in the afternoon. **CLC:** About four o'clock. Lige was on that board, too. Lige Hogge, he was our next-door neighbor for a long time. He was a lawyer and a judge and Commonwealth attorney. He was all those things at one time. This is the group that actually did the working part. Now, my Uncle Cornelius was a great influence in the town. He was the president of People's Bank, and he wanted the hospital very much. It always says that he was president of the foundation. But he was president of the finance committee, actually. And we had the president of the other bank, Glenn Layne, and Alfie Hutchinson. Oh, they all worked, and they had meetings, I think, at least two or three times a week. Then we got to the place where we didn't have to go to those.

SG: *You didn't have to call the meetings, or . . .* **CLC:** When they got to the finance part, you see, they tried—they had to get someone to make the fund drive. We had to get, well, all we figured what we could get, so we had to get somebody to go and get it.

SG: *You said you thought people had pledged $87,000.* **CLC:** I really still have those books. I've got expense books for the first year.

SG: *Did you have an estimate on land and construction, or did you just get the money first?* **CLC:** Actually, the Sisters, they went ahead and planned the building. We bought the land. **SH:** Several people offered land. Because we had the Hill-Burton money, we had to take land in town and we had to buy it. That is, the government, they would double your money. Everybody was involved in that. **CLC:** You had certain rules you had to go by when you used the Hill-Burton money, but I think that's over now. You know, it just lasted so many years. You had to plan to expand, so it really turned out that the land you wanted to buy turned out to be sort of expensive. Now, you know those two houses that are sort of up on the hill and one of them has Santy Claus on it. My Uncle Dave would have given us all of that land for nothing. And then on up the road, just before you turn off for here, where all those pine trees were? Well, where that church is, that's part of the land. Hill-Burton said if people don't have transportation, they can't get out there. People had cars even then. **SH:** But there was no public transportation. **CLC:** But this place worked out all right.

SG: *Was there anything else? Did they have to take anything out?* **SH:** There was a house there, but that's all.

SG: *So how long did it take to get the money?* **CLC:** Oh, we got everything going at the same time. The whole thing was completed in three years.

SG: *Were there ever any cliffhanger moments, like maybe this is not going to happen? Or was it pretty smooth?* CLC: I think it was pretty smooth. Well, there were about a million things that went wrong. I remember, well, we built this place where the doctors' offices were in the hospital, and they wouldn't let us do it. Oh, I tell you. SH: Oh, they threatened Louise—to disbar—I mean, cut her off of the Kentucky Medical Association.

SG: *Could you tell that again? I don't understand.* SH: The doctors' offices in the hospital. They said it was socialistic. Oh, it was terrible, the accusations they made against her. CLC: Oh, I've got two letters I still have. [Laughs]

SG: *You mean, doctors were supposed to have their offices outside the hospital? If so, why?* CLC: Well, I think their philosophy was that they shouldn't be so close that they could be a part of the hospital. The doctor had to be a separate entity, and the hospital had to be another entity. You came to the hospital to work. You weren't a part of the group. SH: That was really a no-no then. CLC: One of my very good friends came down here one day and sat about where you are now, and he just tore me up one side and down the other. [Laughs]

SG: *But for what?* SH: Maybe free enterprise. Maybe that was it. I don't know. CLC: One time somebody was here and he wanted to be a surgeon. And I told him what I said and he said he would do that, but he couldn't do that because nobody would go with him. And I mean, I've always felt we had to get what we need here, and it wasn't, maybe, just exactly fair in the other direction. But we'd get what the community needed. That was our philosophy. If somebody came in and wanted to do their own thing, didn't want to do it our way . . . SH: They were not welcome. They could come, but it was pointed out pretty plain they were not welcome. CLC: You see, we wanted to be sure they were good, and that's why we worked with the University of Kentucky, and when they came they were qualified to teach at the university, to be approved there. And if somebody just came from Podunk and we didn't know 'em, we wanted "top dog" people even though this was a small town, and I still believe this. I believe there's a lot of people that would prefer to live in this kind of an area than in the city, and even if they are smart and rich, they still might like it here. SH: And, you know, I believe Hunter Black is a good example. He was brave to come here, and he came almost in the beginning.

SG: *What do you mean brave?* SH: Let's see, 1961? He came here before Dick Carpenter. You know, they always think that Dick came first, but he didn't come first. CLC: Well, Carpenter came, but then he left.

He had to go into the service. **SH:** And he left and was gone for about three years. **CLC:** They came through the university. I'd say they taught. They had to be part of the staff. **SH:** They were all specialized at the university. And they were welcome to teach there, and all of them did. **CLC:** Not David Victor, but he came down one or two days a week. Let's see, Herb Hudnut was our first medicine man, and he was head of medicine, and he came here with the idea of being the educational supervisor, so to speak. And then Dr. Proudfoot was practicing over at Pikeville, and he came over for about a month, just on Saturdays, as a surgeon, and then after that he became a part of the staff.

SG: *Did you ask him to stay, or did he want to stay?* **CLC:** Oh, he worked with a union or in the mining business. I continued my practice on Main Street. Now we had in town Dr. Blair and Dr. Reynolds and Dr. Jerrett and . . . actually we owned it. That is, if we wanted to, we could put a patient in. And we had a radiologist. I believe Dr. Smith was our first radiologist, and he'd come in. He didn't live here, I don't believe.

SG: *So no doctors' offices were in the hospital?* **CLC:** Actually, I talked to Dr. Willard, and I couldn't see what was wrong with that. And I didn't do a good job. I didn't explain that well. I thought that any fool could see that it was a good plan.

SG: *So you thought they should see that, too?* **CLC:** Yes, but they didn't like that. And that's when I got that letter. Anyhow, we just moved 'em out, and they got a little house next door, and that was the end of that. That just became a part of the hospital.

SG: *Is that how the Morehead Clinic got started?* **CLC:** That was the beginning. That was a clinic. Then it was a clinic that wanted to divide itself, so it divided into two clinics.

SG: *That sounds like another chapter. So in the meantime the hospital was in the hands of the Sisters and you were . . . ?* **CLC:** Outside. Oh, I've been on the board ever since, and I'm still on the board.

SG: *When they started building the hospital—well, I've been curious about this ever since I've been here. This is such a Protestant area, and the hospital is Catholic and run by Sisters. Was there any noise about that?* **SH:** Do you mean did people object? There was a lot less objection than you'd think. **CLC:** It was really surprising. We had two churches that weren't really for us. **SH:** In fact, one minister in the beginning was an opponent. He changed a lot. He changed before the hospital was completed. And that was about John Kennedy's time, and I remember he wrote a letter to the editor about Kennedy and the hospital. He was one of the folks, but he came around just fine. **CLC:** An important member of each of those churches was in the hospital within the first week. I don't know exactly when, but it was very shortly after. As I say, they didn't think, they didn't reason. It was just luck, chance, being at the right place at the right time. Those are things that count. **SH:** We had a great advantage in that it was the right time for the hospital. And the university was expanding, and we got so much help. **CLC:** And the university up here could see the need of it. You see, they were trying to grow, too. You couldn't get good teachers if you couldn't get good health facilities.

SG: *You mean Dr. Doran?* **CLC:** Well, UK, but Dr. Doran, too, and we had it both ways.

SG: *Did you think of that when you would sit up nights discussing your plans?* **CLC:** No, we just didn't know how we were going to get doctors. I tell you, it was just plain luck that this man happened to sit down by me.

SG: *How did you try to attract doctors to Morehead itself? What if they said they didn't want to live in a little town?* **SH:** Well, we tried to point out the attractive points and the university and the things kids can do here. At that time an awful lot of young children came to the university because of Breckinridge Training School. Of course, Breck is no more. **CLC:** But that was a selling point.

SG: *In James McConkey's book [Rowan's Progress], he said that he thought you might have built this house like this so that doctors coming here would think they could have a house like this.* **CLC:** Well, we had to entertain them, and we didn't want them to feel like they were going into a log cabin. **SH:** You just wouldn't believe the wining and dining. Oh! **CLC:** Yes, I can remember hypertension in that room over there, wining all over the place. But we tried to show them that you can do whatever you want to do. **SH:** I mean we did all of that—we, meaning me. **CLC:** She did. We'd have twenty-five people and more here for dinner at one time. **SH:** Oh, more than that. I mean, we had a place here and a place there and anyplace there was a chair, and we'd bring more in. I do not know how we did it. This is after working all day, oh, yes. We do not know how we did all that. **CLC:** We didn't have time to shop even.

SG: *So did it work?* **CLC:** We think we got a good bunch. **SH:** And we got to know them a little bit. Some of them really didn't want it. But it worked, and that was how we did it. Other people entertained, too. I remember Jane had people a few times and Norma Hogge did.

SG: *So you wanted them to know that Morehead could be a good experience.* **CLC:** And that they could talk [to the people] and that they had read a few books.

SG: *When they finally opened the hospital in 1963, I read somewhere that the first premature birth in the hospital was in the first year. Were you involved in that?* **SH:** Yes, we were, I think. I don't know if you delivered it or Billie Jo Caudill did. But I know that we took care of it a lot. Billie Jo was in the office at that time. Yes, she was involved.

SG: *So, as soon as it opened, you did all your deliveries there. Was that a good feeling?* **CLC:** Oh, yes. Oh, we thought we were in hog heaven. **SH:** Why, you could stay home after that. Didn't have to wait for that baby and stay all night. **CLC:** We lived in that office then. **SH:** But they had a bell and they could ring, but you still had to check every so often.

SG: *In what year had you built that office?* **SH:** In 1957. Nine years. **CLC:** That's many a year.

SG: *When they opened the hospital and they named it St. Claire, how did that come about?* **CLC:** Well, the Sisters named it. Oh, it was down at the office, and I think Sister Joelle . . . **SH:** Well, some of them—I think Dr. Segnitz wanted to call it the Morehead Hospital or Morehead Medical Center, because everything was medical center then, as it is now. That was okay. And then we talked about St. Francis of Assisi, and St. Claire was right there. You know, she took care of sick people, and that's how it came about, and Louise's first name is Claire. **CLC:** I think it was Mother Borromeo. **SH:** That was it. She just decided that that would be the name. The people agreed, you know. It was after everybody agreed—which was the Sisters and Dr. Segnitz—that's about it. It was just a small group. I mean, it wasn't but six or seven people. **CLC:** It was really peculiar to me. It really was. **SH:** And the committees worked really well. I mean, committees so often don't work so well. But these did.

SG: *Maybe because they had a real purpose. Often committees don't have a reason for existing at all. But the impetus to build a hospital—do you think that's why?* **SH:** And Crutcher helped a lot, no doubt about it. I mean, you have to have publicity, and he did a fine job.

SG: *Who was mayor then?* **SH:** Probably Bill Layne.

SG: *When they did the first groundbreaking, were you there?* **CLC:** Oh, yes. **SH:** Every time there is a groundbreaking, almost.

SG: *Now, everyone believes the hospital is named after you.* **SH:** It is.

SG: *When you knew that, how did you feel?* **CLC:** I don't know how I feel. There's something wrong with my feeling state. I had pretty much to do with it, and it needed a name and, oh . . . **SH:** Well, being named a Saint somebody when it's a Catholic hospital . . . **CLC:** That's part of it.

SG: *Do you think, when you look back, it was as they say on this St. Claire calendar. It was a dream, a vision, a fairy tale?* **CLC:** Yes, well, it was a dream. I mean, you had to sort of put your stuff together. You couldn't, as I say, you couldn't figure it out. You just had to—everything happened about as good as it could have, in my opinion, as good as you could expect. We had lucky breaks.

Ellie Reser
January 18, 1993

Mrs. Ellie Reser, R.N., is now the chaplain/bereavement coordinator for the St. Claire Medical Center. She is almost as beloved in Morehead as Dr. Louise. Mrs. Reser came to Morehead from Indiana as a young bride and new nurse and worked in Louise and Susie's office. She began the local hospice program. Her explanations of how Dr. Louise works as a healer are probably the closest clues to be found for Dr. Louise's special magic.

Ellie Reser was the organizing energy behind the seventh-fifth birthday celebration for Dr. Louise and was prepared with letters and pictures and a script for the play she had written for that occasion.

Louise's history is rather interwoven with the history of the university, and the reason for that is that she and Bob Bishop and that little group of children used to play in a playhouse which is just where the University Center is now. She also was on the faculty at Morehead before she went to medical school. During the war they taught sailors here. I believe they were trying to make instant officers all over the United States, teaching people math and things that they could use in being navigators and that sort of thing. So during the early years of the war they had military men on campus. But it was in the late forties, I think, that Louise went back to medical school. She finished faster than normal because the physician shortage was so great at that time. So she did what would normally take people four and a half years in less time. I can't imagine how much studying that must take to do what she did.

The way I know some of the stories about Louise is that we had this little sort of celebration of her life, and it was to coincide with her forty years of practice in Morehead. And it was also a celebration of the hospital. They wanted to do something to honor her. They asked me to think about a script for what we should do at that celebration. What I did to prepare for that was to find as many people as I could that went to high school with her—because she went all of her years in school right here in Rowan County, except when she went away to college and med school. And Bob Bishop was forthcoming, and Jane [Mrs. Boone Caudill], her sisters, and several other people I have listed in that script. And I asked them to come together at the hospital for a luncheon, just to tell stories. It was wonderful. We took down the stories and, as I listened, I took down stories that I thought would play.

One of the most wonderful stories that is the most fun to do was when the children, making adventure for themselves, they put a pony in the third-floor window of what was then the Evans home. The Evans home was a center of a lot of their activities. One of her dearest friends was Sidney Evans. And her brother "Tick" Evans is still living. Now he didn't remember too much about putting the pony up there, but Mr. Cassity did. Bob Bishop did. And how they ever got that pony up three flights of stairs? Well, when Mrs. Evans got home from one of the church meetings—the Methodist church was about two blocks away—she saw this pony looking out of the window and a lot of people in the yard. That was one of their best stories.

Another story I tried to get them to talk about is what she did scholastically. Did she compete in anything? And she and Bob Bishop were competing on the debate team. I guess the farthest point they would have gone would have been over to West Liberty, but in those days the roads were so terrible that you had to go on the train. From what I understand, you had to go out to where Lee Clay was to get on the train. . . . That was a brick manufacturing place. That's where the North Fork Railroad was, and that railroad would take you up to just outside of West Liberty. But you would have to spend the night because that train went so infrequently, and then they would walk home from Clearfield. There was another hangout that was for young people, and that was the Old Eagle's Nest. It was where Arby's is now, and there used to be the Midland Trail Hotel. Up from that was the Eagle's Nest. It was known in this area for many, many years as the place to eat between Ashland and Lexington. See, back in those days you had to travel on U.S. 60, and it was an all-day trip practically to go from Ashland to Lexington because the roads were curvy and two-lane all the way. So this was a good place to stop and eat lunch. The food was excellent.

When I first came to Morehead, the Eagle's Nest was the place to go. In the morning men would all sit around this huge round table and you could find out the news of the day that way. The women would usually stop by for coffee in the afternoon. And they would sometimes bring their little children with them and they would sit over on the side—there were little tiny tables for them—and they would sip Coke while the women exchanged the news of the street. We used [in the skits] just one little thing with the Eagle's Nest and tried to incorporate dances of the day, which would have been the Charleston and those things.

Louise was always sort of at the center of a lot of activities, she and her sister, Cille [Lucille Caudill Little]. Cille, to this day, is very vibrant and expressive. And I can imagine that she and Louise together would have been quite an interesting pair. They are very close in age, I think next to each other in age.

Now, Jane Caudill was Louise's brother's wife—Boone. She and Boone and their father were involved with the bank in Sandy Hook, as is Boone Proctor Caudill. They still are. Louise is also on the board. Their names are synonymous with banking. [Louise's father, Daniel Boone Caudill, also helped found People's Bank in Morehead.]

Louise's people were so vital to the development of this area that I would think that some of this is important to tell you about Louise because the banks in Morehead and Elliot County and maybe in one other place were all founded by her father's brothers. Daniel Boone, her father, was at Sandy Hook. There was a brother that was with a People's Bank here, and so there was a story that they told me one time which I did not record. But it was about how they first brought the money, which was to start the bank at Morehead, over the ridge. They brought it, I think the story goes, in bags of meal that they were bringing over here. See, it was kind of rough and woolly down where Highway 32 is now. And the stories that I have read about the Rowan County War and the way things were is that that was a place you went through when it was good to know somebody who knew somebody along the way. Because, you know, there were people that really wanted your possessions—not just to do you harm. But it was kind of a rough place.

However, in the midst of all this roughness, there was also a great deal of culture. And I think that the Evanses and the Caudills, all of these good solid families, kind of first settlers that you talk about from Rowan County, they paid attention to education. I mean, Louise graduated from Columbia in New York City. I believe her family cared a lot about what we would think good moral values are. I know they did because they had been good, upstanding business people as long as I can remember. They went to the church of Phoebe Button and her son—that came to make Morehead Normal School. They were sort of like missionaries in their view of coming here. I'm not sure that Brother Button wasn't a minister in the Christian church. That may show up in George Young's paper. In fact, I'm sort of giving you—oh, I don't want this to be a historical document.

Well, they tried to tell me at the time I was doing the stories that "Tick" Evans was a little bit older. His name is really Eldon Evans—but I think he would surely fill you in on how the Evans family and the Caudill family were close. It may be that they are somehow related. Louise's family is such a large family—they came out of Poplar Grove. I was once visiting a home health patient out there. They said, "Do you know Dr. Louise Caudill?" I said, "Yes, I do." They said, "Do you know that this is where her father grew up?" It's out right on the line between Elliot and Morgan. It's a beautiful area. There's a ridge that goes along and they lived down in this house rather down a steep hill. I believe that—I know they sold meal and maybe things like that [farmed].

What I'm trying to say is that her family and some other good solid families in this community made a foundation for what Morehead has become today. Because the town of Owingsville, Mt. Sterling, and these other places seemed like they had more money, and you will find the big fine old homes there. These people didn't have that kind of money, but they had the values and the foresight to see that some things would happen here and would happen right.

And Louise has been a mover in that direction. You know, she taught at school, but she—well, it was kind of unheard of for a woman her age, if you already had a profession, to go back to school and put in all that time at medical school, which couldn't have been easy. And back then, women doctors were very scarce. They were looked on as an oddity. Jane is the one who can tell you about how they started the office there in that building above the pool hall. Granny Caudill owned that building. Louise's mother. Everybody called her "Granny Caudill." She was much loved by the community. As she grew older she drove a great big Cadillac right down the middle of the street! She *might* stop at Second Street, but, then again, she might not. And we all knew her. It was a small town. This town has grown so much just since the time I've come here. But she was a much loved woman. So gracious, inviting everyone to her home.

I think Louise's gregariousness came from both sides of the family. From her father, who could politic with the best of them. But her mother had that sort of all-encompassing thing to sort of help the world and did a lot with the church and all. Her mom came from, I believe, lawyers. The Proctors. I'm quite sure that two of her mother's brothers read law. They were all interested in education. I think at that time for them to have aspirations for their daughter to become a doctor—well! Louise has said that her father told her that she could be anything she wanted to be. Now, for Mr. Dan Caudill to say that back in those days, I think, was just remarkable.

We kept trying to have the hospital here—and everyone kept telling us that we didn't have enough of a population base. And this was not a Catholic town. I could say that we could name for you the Catholics. There were ten or less, and they met in a little garage church up near the old swimming pool, where their church is now. And Susie was a part of that congregation. Well, the local people called on the Baptists, and they weren't interested, and the Methodists, and they weren't. I was so pleased that in their planning they didn't try to make it a little county hospital because it could never have become what it is now.

Louise's vision and the vision of the early leaders was that we would have a hospital of quality with specialists. And I believe that, even in those early days, Louise was looking for university links. Because she did not want this just to be a little lying-in hospital. This was to be someplace where we did competitive medicine. We could get all the right tests here without going to Lexington.

When this hospital got started, the Appalachian Regional Commission was taking over. The miners' hospitals were down in southeastern Kentucky, and they were putting little hospitals in just everywhere, and they were spreading out into every little community. Well, the communities were without medical care. But in the planning stages, they were just willing to put up a building, and somehow it would be staffed. And Louise and her group realized that this was going to get them in trouble. I mean, if you are going to have a hospital, you have to have competent people in lab and X ray, and you can't just bring in individual doctors. You have to have things to help them do their work. So it was her vision that we wouldn't go with something we couldn't really do a fine job with.

Louise Caudill has never been happy with anything that wasn't good quality. That shows in her schooling, that shows in her practice. For example, their records are exemplary. Louise kept good records when those around us didn't, even when she wasn't wanting to be with Medicaid. When Medicaid first came out, it was a mess. There were some people really cashing in with it. And they got indicted because they had no records to say what they had, no records to back up what they were charging for. Louise's records down there starting in 1957—for me—she can look back and see everything that has happened to me since 1957. It's right there. And you could think that, as she grew older, she wouldn't pay as much attention to that, but they are just as meticulous today as she and Susie were on the very first day I went to see them. I had my second child in that office down there.

Now, here's how my life crossed Louise's: I was a brand-new graduate from the Lutheran Hospital School of Nursing back in 1957. That was in Fort Wayne, Indiana. I was from a little town just south of Fort Wayne. My husband at that time had graduated from Morehead State Teachers' College. He was from Indiana. He had come down here on a music scholarship and also did theatre. He knew Louise very well at that time because they supported the theatre, even back then. Every production he was in, I'm sure Louise and Susie were there. There was no place for me to work in Morehead. There were three doctors, and they already had a nurse. The health department had a nurse. And I can remember how just really forlorn I felt. I had been offered a really good position at my own hospital because I'd graduated with honors. And I thought, "Where in the world am I going?" I must have been twenty-one, and my husband was going to go to graduate school and expected to get his degree in one year.

His degree would have been in education, but his undergraduate was theatre/music. His name was Don Holloway. They have a scholarship named for him now. Anyway, he came home one day and said, "I've found a job for you. It's in a little town named Olive Hill. You can be the nurse at this Methodist boarding school." I was pretty excited. It was imperative that I work because Don was in school and we had no money.

Well, I did take that job in Olive Hill, and the superintendent left, and the principal of the school got drafted, and that was during the Korean conflict, and that left the school without a principal. Well, Don had enough credits, graduate education credits, so they said he could have an emergency certificate so that he could keep the kids' grades that year. But the Methodist church had already begun to say that they were going to phase out the school because it was originally meant for mountain children who couldn't afford to get to school otherwise. That was before a lot of school busing. So they came and boarded, and the families could come on weekends, and at vacation time they could go home. As I remember, there were about forty boarding students and sixty day students. I still remember my very difficult year in Olive Hill.

Well, there were marches on the school. They were going to close that school. People were angry about it, very angry. They padlocked the buildings and did all kinds of threatening. They thought the school should stay open and that the Methodist church had done the people wrong. Well, it was a terrible year. No violence, but some days the drunks would be shooting so that some days I wouldn't hang out the wash. They'd be shooting up in the trees.

The problem was that the Carter County schools were, at that time, in such bad shape that they really did worry about sending their kids to school. See, that was the time when the brickyards were there. Harbison Walker and General Refractories were at full speed, and they had superintendents of these places, and they were from Pennsylvania. It would be like bringing someone to Morehead if our schools were really bad. And there was no culture or whatever. These people thought we were taking their center of culture, their center of education, and so they were very angry. And, of course, we were the local people put there by the Methodist Mission Board.

All that doesn't have anything to do with Louise except to say that when we moved to Morehead the next year, I felt like I was coming to heaven because I could go into town and people talked to me. There, in the banks sometimes, we wouldn't be waited on! And one drugstore in Olive Hill we couldn't go to because they would just say ugly things. I worked a little bit over there with a young physician who left after two years. It was an angry town. So I came to Morehead where there was a university and I had a physician. I think my first entry on my card with Louise was for my oral polio, and that would have been back in 1957. I knew immediately when I met her that this lady was going to be my doctor.

Louise was a little, very athletic person. She played a lot of tennis. She was very up when you talked to her. One thing was that she had a more family-oriented practice, and the other thing was that my husband had gone to her as a student. She was the one to whom more students went than any place else.

You know, all those doctors were cousins. Dr. Blair's mother was Daniel Boone Caudill's sister—grew up right here, so they were close, by being relatives. And then Sam Reynolds was also a cousin, but I'm not sure exactly how that worked, but all three were related. Well, in those times, you lived with people in your county. They had large families, and you didn't go away; you stayed there. So they intermarried. Anyway, my husband thought so highly of Louise, and so, of course, that's where I went.

She had just moved into her brand-new place. The same buildings were around here then. That apartment building has been there for a real long time. A little bit later I worked as the office nurse for Billie Jo Caudill, who was a second cousin who practiced with Louise for a while. But it didn't work out. You know, when there's an established practice—and Louise knew everybody so well, it was very hard for the people to say, "Well, Billie Jo will be your doctor." They wanted Louise and Susie. I worked in their office. I actually worked for Billie Jo—this was a woman—so Louise and Susie would work in the morning and Billie Jo and I worked in the afternoon. And then we would alternate. Both of them did a lot of deliveries there in the office. And then it was during this time or shortly after I started working for Billie Jo that the hospital was being planned.

I worked for Billie Jo for three years. We stayed with Louise, I think, for about nine months or so, and then we set up an office just up the street. See, I was a known quantity that had no job here. And there just weren't very many nurses here. Now that was something we thought about also when we were building the hospital. Where are we going to get the nurses?

I wouldn't say it was a competition, because Louise's people were not leaving and Louise had more than enough to do. And she had another young man that came and worked with her and it was the same thing. People wanted Louise; they didn't want anybody else. I think that happens, probably, in practices that are already established and a new person comes. But these people are very loyal and honor that physician, and they don't want another one. I'm sure if *we* told patients to do something they would first call up Susie to make sure it was the right thing to do.

I am a very loyal patient of Louise's, even though I worked for a while for this other physician. Oh, I liked Louise immediately. I think that when you go to see Louise, well, she makes you feel like you are the only one in the world that she's concerned about. I can't imagine anyone thinking that she had anything else on her mind; she does that. And how do people have this ability? I just don't know.

I also go to a specialist now. But when I have to go and get myself adjusted mentally, I walk down the street to Louise. She sometimes gives me a prescription, but I don't really need any pills usually, because by the time I have left her I have things in perspective. And I've had some really difficult things happen in my life. She has known all about them. She has always been there. No matter when I had to call, no matter how upset I was, she would make some kind of order out of it. And out of so much of what happened that she's been entwined with, she became a friend more than anything else. She still is a friend. She is a friend that knows how to put my psyche back to square one. I go there—not very often—probably every six or eight months—whenever I need an adjustment. I always have some little physical complaint, but then it always gets down to the fact that I never get sick if I don't have something bothering me inside.

I think my breast cancer came from a lot of the incredible stress that I was under with my parents. So, yes, if you are stressed, your body shows it in many ways. Louise has been touting this—that stress causes illness—for as long as I've known her. And that was way before they wrote about it. And she always had made sure, in talking with us and having us point out what was going on in our life at that time, that it generally has something to do with what's happening with us then. That has been true for me. You could look back through my cards at her office and the illnesses. For example, at one time of strain, I ended up in St. Joe's Hospital with a disease they couldn't figure out. My immune system went crazy, and I had knots on my legs and all sorts of things. They treated me with things. But when we came back and Louise and I sorted it out, my body had finally just said, "It's too much stress." So I ended up in a bed for six weeks, and I got well.

She doesn't say that to you. No, she lets *you* say it. She is an adept counselor. She never has to say it to you. She works you around until you say it yourself. And that's the height of counseling. To bring that realization to the person—saying this is what is wrong with you or this is what to do—she more than likely will say, "Well, let's talk about it. We can do this or we can do that. But maybe, now that you know what's going on, maybe we should just see if it's going to settle down by itself." This has happened to me just in the last month. She said, "I think we might identify what's causing it." Which is totally emotional, and she said, "Usually when you find out what it is that seems to be doing it for you, it doesn't take much medicine for you." And that's the truth. I took the pills back to Susie and said, "I don't think I need these. I think I'm going to try other things. It's going to take awhile." And they are fine about that. That's the way they like to see it.

One thing I want to mention is the incredible way that she and Susie work hand in glove. I saw it firsthand when I worked there. It was amazing. Susie knew what Louise was going to do practically before Louise did it. It is sort of like a beautiful dance. Susie has this whole role of things that she manages, and she is the one who reminds Louise when someone needs a Pap smear or when to order a chest X ray. Susie is the best physician's assistant that I know. She is able to sort out the emotional things with people she knows when it's time that you have to talk to Louise. She never tries to keep you from seeing Louise. But I know that when they would be seeing pages and pages of people in that office and delivering babies. . . . I don't know how Susie kept things going. I don't know how they made it.

They didn't get very much rest in their early days. The hospital did help that some, because that way the nurses could watch the patients until they had to be called in. But before that, when somebody came in [in labor], Susie was up checking them. She had to. I had a delivery at Bellefont Hospital in Ashland for my first child. But my second delivery was the best. And I went in at 12:30 p.m. of that day. I took castor oil at 5:30 in the morning. It's good for you if you are overdue. So I went there at 12:30 and had the baby at 2:30 p.m. and went home at 6:00 p.m.

And Susie was marvelous. I think I had two whiffs of chloroform and that was it. I was awake and the baby cried before she was even fully out of the birth canal. I always tease Rachel that she came out hollering and has been talking ever since. I walked to the delivery table. Louise would take your arm, kind of help you, but she would say, "Now you have to walk.

Now you've got to move." And she'd sling your arm over her shoulder and, buddy, you walked and got on that table. I remember Susie saying, "Louise, you don't have time." Turn around, and Rachel was there. But what if she had come that fast and I was on my way to Lexington? That's scary!

It was a perfect delivery. I went home that day. It was like what they say are new kinds of things today—birthing centers. Louise had one years ago, before they wrote about them. And she had an emergency room that was available. She always said, "God has been good to us. We didn't lose any mothers." And she said, "We were so far away from help." She knew the risks. But it was better than doing it at home because she had more help there in the office than you would have up the creek somewhere. But she knew that [the birthing center] wasn't the end, and I believe that that was a great impetus for the hospital. She did not want to lose a mother. I think that would have killed her if, because she didn't have enough help, she lost somebody. I think that was one of her great worries.

You think about it. Years back, some of the times they went up a "holler" so then they couldn't see any other patients. So bringing them to their own birthing center helped a lot. The idea of a real hospital was something she talked about from early on.

Louise, I think, has suffered from insomnia some, and instead of doing things like most people do, I think—drinking warm milk or whatever—Louise gets up and she ponders and reads. She reads medical journals. Probably one of the best-read physicians in this town. She reads all the new things. And apparently she does not require a great deal of sleep because she always was saying things like, "Well, I was up wandering about the other night, and I got to thinking about . . ." Also, I think she was seeing cases that I think she felt like could be taken care of here. And I believe that it was probably out of these night time musings that she thought, "Why can't we have a hospital here?" But it was at that time that she also said, "And it's not going to be one of these little two-bit hospitals." She always has practiced careful medicine. She would not be happy with one that wasn't excellent. And so it's now a matter of record as to what she did. And James McConkey wrote about that [in *Rowan's Progress*]—he really did a wonderful job. Especially concerning the complexities of getting a hospital here. And there were problems.

Do you remember John F. Kennedy? Do you remember how some people thought that the pope was going to ruin us? It was back then, it was the same milieu, same period of time, 1961-1963. It was the Kennedy years. People were very exercised about having a Catholic president and the loss of religious freedom. We heard, oh, terrible things. It was bad, the things we heard. Some would have preferred no hospital to having Catholics. It was that strong. The feeling was that bad.

One of our favorite stories is about this gentleman who got up in a prayer meeting and said, "I don't know about anybody else, but if I ever get sick, don't stop at this Catholic hospital. Just put me in an ambulance and take me on to Central Baptist in Lexington." Well, as luck would have it, this same gentleman fell down the stairs in the winter during a snowstorm and broke his hip. He was more than happy to go to the St. Claire Medical Center. There he was attended to most carefully by the good Sisters. We had a lot of Sisters at that time. And Dr. Warren Proudfoot fixed his hip, and he was cared for beautifully. And after it was over, he testified about the good care he received.

In the early days, when we did have the hospital, "Snooks" Crutcher, the newspaper editor, he'd write these columns. Well, he loved the Sisters. He adored Sister Mary Edwin. But he wrote explanations in the newspaper about how we were to address them and about what Sisters were, because in this area people were totally ignorant about those things and about the Sisters. He told about the ones who would be nurses and who would be lab techs. See, all the major parts of the hospital were supervised in the first years by a nun. And they all had the expertise that we needed. Now, we had some Hill-Burton money, government money. The Sisters made a considerable investment. I really don't know how it all worked financially.

The Sisters of Notre Dame are from Covington, Kentucky. They are mostly teaching Sisters. In fact, when we had this hospital, they had a nursing home in St. Charles—St. Charles in Covington. That and this place are their only two medical facilities. They had had a little hospital in Lynch, but that closed. That was just prior to coming here, and they may have had an investment in the St. Charles nursing home, and they weren't looking for a job.

But Monsignor Towell was the one that pushed them. And word was that he called the Sisters and gave them the word that they needed help here. That story that he saw those babies lined up on the couch. And that was just by accident. We just don't know. He just showed up. Louise and Susie didn't know he was coming. He'd just said that he would stop some time when he came through here. And on the day he came was when we had all these babies. And Susie had them all lined up on the couch, I think. When the monsignor saw that, he was just, just so touched. Because, here are these babies that need a place, that need a hospital. He just couldn't imagine that they were here with not any more than that. He thought they should have a nursery like a hospital.

And this is the thing that we credit it with—some act of providence that he came to Morehead on the same day that all those babies got here. And that his heart was very touched by babies that he felt should have been in a hospital nursery. The truth is, those babies were probably just fine. I know they had been cared for very well. But the monsignor saw this was a place where he felt the Notre Dames ought to come. Five babies all born on the same night is kind of stupefying.

I don't know who those five babies were. We tried to find some of them. We tried [for that program] finding all the first babies—the first baby in the hospital we got. We did a lot of sleuthing. And that night of the celebration for Louise, I was so choked I couldn't possibly sing, because all of those babies, now grown people— and one of mine was up there holding hands. They encircled the Button Auditorium. At least a thousand people sang "We Are the World, We Are Your Children."

Louise knew about the celebration. She was kind of, well, oh, well, kind of self-effacing. She thought, oh, maybe a couple hundred people would show up. That place was full. I've never seen Button as full.

She loved it. She finally came, and we had all the people who told us the stories, and we had kind of an honor section right there, and she was right there seated in the middle, and we had a reception for her afterwards. This celebration isn't the same thing as you are doing. This was just a tribute to her, but this has to be more. I think this has so much to do with what a difference a life can make to a community.

Her history, yes, we know some of that, but I believe a great deal should be put into the way she is able to look at a patient as a total person. She has always practiced holistic medicine, before it was even known. She started a birthing center before people even talked about it. She was ahead of her time in many, many things. For example, these stress-related things. She's always been there and she's always been reading and trying to be the best she could be. She would have been a healer no matter where or when she was born. I feel that she is the essence of the traditional women healers that I've read about. And women healers bring a different energy to medicine than men do. I'm talking about women's traditional role as being a nurturer as well as, or along with, the healing process. And I feel that Louise has brought an extra energy to this healing.

I'm looking at her from her point of view. I'm looking at it as a woman healer; looking at the total environment and realizing, right up front, that many people come to the doctor's office for emotional needs instead of real physical needs. The two are entwined and that somebody who has the gift of eliciting information that will help her be able to help the patient. As I said before, she works you around until you are able to identify what the problem is. You don't wait for her to say, "This is what I think and this is what I'm going to give you for it." You work out your own plan. I've been working out plans for myself with her for many years. Not always did it mean that I did them! Changes, things that would make me healthier. Sometimes it could be a dietary change, but she has not loaded me up with tranquilizers. Louise has only given me short-term things. She hasn't been pushing pills. She has been pushing insight into your own problems, like what changes you can make. There's a lot of good counseling that goes into her practice, and I think that that's why she is such a good healer.

Now, this happens with everybody. I send people to her when I think that basically that is what they need—that they need to go and talk to somebody that can gently lead them. She kind of gently brings them around. I've sent many disturbed college students to Louise Caudill, and they've come back much better.

I think she just genuinely loves people and wants to help them. Well, you see, people that you know really do make a difference, and I think it shows up all the time in medicine because you yourself can know if, when you go to the doctor, for something—are they really listening to you? She's not the only physician that has this gift, but I feel like she has used her gift longer and more successfully than many other people.

When I think of Louise Caudill, I think of a healer, in the very best sense of the term. I know that with Louise it is an internal thing. It comes from within. It's not something she's studied to learn how to do. She has studied medicine and she went to good medical schools. However, I believe that, as with teaching and with many other professions, there is something, sometimes, a gift that people will have.

Louise was born with her gift to heal. And Susie has a great gift, too, and I think about it a lot. Susie has always been the support system. She never tried being a star. And she has worked in the background facilitating, making the rough way smooth. She's a great cook. I think she could see whenever Louise needed positive reinforcement. When things were going bad, she'd have people to dinner. Still, she was running the office, getting up in the night to go along out on calls. Susie has been a very, very great part of this team. And I believe that Susie is bright. She is very, very bright. When I come in, Susie knows me and I just say, "I don't think it's an antibiotic that I need. I need to speak with Louise." And she's so kind. You know, I love Susie, and I feel she has offered me as much healing in many ways by facilitating.

Dr. Claire Louise Caudill and Susie Halbleib
February 13, 1993

This interview began with a list of questions about details but went in several directions. What shines through is that Dr. Louise and Susie were two people with the same goal—in their words, "to make medicine count for something."

SG: *It is interesting to show the town-and-gown atmosphere that is Morehead. Was it more so then? Do you think the school grew because of the hospital?* **CLC:** Surely was a factor in it. It went two ways, trying to get physicians in. They had to have places for their children to go to school. Our university had a training school at the time we were planning this [hospital], so that was a big drawing card for getting doctors. In the same way, the university was having a hard time getting faculty because there was no medical facility. It really was a cooperative sort of thing and it worked well. And I think everybody saw the value of the two.

SG: *Today I have a list of questions that are all over the place, so I might jump around. Also, I interviewed Ellie Reser because she is so involved with health in this area and you may not want to comment on her comment, but I thought I'd just ask you. She said, "Louise is a healer." That there are doctors and there are medical people and there are real healers and you are one of those, the healers. I see you smiling . . .* **CLC:** Oh, I know what she's saying. I think a lot of people come to a doctor just to talk. **SH:** I agree. They do! And Louise is good at that. She can get people to talk to her about their problems, their illnesses.

SG: *Which sort of leads to the next question, which is—and people say this more and more today—that your mind and body are totally connected, that you can make up your mind not to let your leg let you fall.* **SH:** Well, I think, I agree, the mind is a big factor in any ailment, whether it's physical or a combination. Most everything is a combination.

SG: *Do you think people can just give up?* **CLC:** Did you ever notice how many people, if their spouse dies, within six months they die? **SH:** Even if the other spouse wasn't sick, they get sick.

SG: *So what you say—your mind, does it grasp what you are saying if you say it.* **CLC:** Yes, if you say it or feel it even.

SG: *Often I hear students say ahead of time, "I won't do well" or "I'm no good." So, as a healer, just knowing that and letting people talk it out is a healing part?* **CLC:** I think you have to get everything together and compare it all. You just have to figure things out. Sort of lead them along, you know. They can almost always give you pretty good examples from what has happened.

SG: *How did you come to know this?* **CLC:** I guess it was in course 404. [Laughs.] No, there is no course in med school.

SG: *Anyone who knows what I'm trying to do says, "Oh, I love Dr. Louise. And let me tell you this, and I must tell you that." Everybody loves you. How does that make you feel?* **CLC:** I guess I'm just a good liar.

SG: *What?* **CLC:** A good liar. Makes everybody feel good. Oh, I don't win everybody.

SG: *What is your general feeling about people?* **CLC:** I believe I like people. I like people to be their own self. I don't like people to try to play like they are something else. I like them to do their own thing. Oh, I like for people to like me. Well, Susie and I were talking about this on our way home from a funeral recently—that there was the age when people really did think a lot of us because that's when we were going out to homes and we just carried everybody's problems. We carried everybody's problems, didn't we? But the people there [at the funeral home on this day] were about that older age group.

SG: *Did getting the hospital going and growing sort of leave you less close?* **SH:** Well, there's just so much you can do. There is no way we can go on and work as hard as we used to. **CLC:** No, we can't do that.

SG: *We've never talked about how people paid you or what they paid you with.* **CLC:** We had one man come in about two or three years ago and pay us for five babies. **SH:** Not with interest, but at least they did think to do that.

SG: *Five? What would you charge at first? You were telling me about going out to cabins. Did they ask you what you charged, or did you have a flat fee?* **CLC:** I think we started at thirty-five or fifty dollars. **SH:** We started at fifty dollars. Now that meant prenatal care, delivery, and one home call after delivery. **CLC:** We got rich!

SG: *No matter how difficult it was to get there?* **SH:** Sometimes it would maybe be four or five days after if they lived a long ways, because then we'd go out on Saturday afternoon.

SG: *And if they couldn't pay you?* **SH:** We always went, and Louise never did look at the books, ever. She still doesn't. It's not her line. And I've never fussed at people for not paying. **CLC:** But if they smoked a lot of cigarettes, Susie'd fuss at them. **SH:** Oh, I'd tell 'em how much cigarettes cost and if you'd stop smoking you could put this much back. And I used to figure out in dollars and cents how much they could save and they could pay for having this baby. It didn't work, but I did it. **CLC:** But, you know, that's not even a worry in my mind—ever in my life, and I guess I'm really fortunate. I always had a checkbook.

SG: *Do you think that made a difference?* **CLC:** It may have. I mean, I don't know how it would be otherwise.

SG: *I wonder sometimes if people don't think that doctors are out for the money and they make a lot of money. Or do doctors feel they need to make a lot of money?* **CLC:** Well, remember, it costs a lot to do what you have to do.

SG: *All that equipment must be terribly expensive.* **SH:** Oh, it's unbelievable. Unbelievable. **CLC:** We just wrote checks for all our X-ray machines and there it was. **SH:** Back then [in the 1940s], the X-ray machine—and it's unbelievable—cost $5,000. At that time it was a tremendous amount. **CLC:** Now, with an X-ray machine they'll try to tell you—oh, you can make that money back in no time if you'll just X-ray everything. Well, we didn't have time to just fiddle with X ray. We only X-rayed if we had to. **SH:** Sometimes they didn't pay for it anyhow.

SG: *Was it more common than not—that people couldn't pay?* **CLC:** They paid for it when they could. After the war it was pretty prosperous. **SH:** The university people paid, but we'd send them to Lexington because they could afford to go.

SG: *How do I say this? When you hear something like this, it sounds as if you had decided to dedicate yourselves to taking care of the poor. However, when I talk with you, I don't hear that. I just hear that you took care of people.* **SH:** I think that's very good—taking care of sick people.

SG: *Did you ever get paid in odd things like chickens or quilts?* **CLC:** I don't think we ever did. **SH:** People bring us things all the time. More like presents. Now, you take this rug. That one over there, the woven rug. A ninety-year-old man made that. **CLC:** Yes, everybody talks about getting paid in odd. Well, we never did that. We never did that. If you couldn't pay us, you couldn't pay us. That $3.47 was the worst one. It was a delivery and they had saved all the time this woman had been pregnant in order to be able to pay for the delivery. So at the time she delivered they had saved $3.47. They insisted that we take it. They didn't want us to do that for nothing. That was one of those places, I told you, where they didn't have any floor, just the ground. They had no water, no light, nothing. But the child had a bladder that was on the outside. It lived. We sent it to Lexington.

SG: *What do you think, in your time working with patients and medicine and reading, are the best medical advances in your lifetime?* **CLC:** It would have to be technology, I think. **SH:** Another thing, when we started out, people died of tuberculosis and cancer of the cervix. It's rare that happens anymore. We actually saw people die of tuberculosis complications. And we saw many women with cancer of the cervix. You just don't see much now. I mean, people do still die of cancer of the cervix, but to me those are few. Pap smears account for that and having examinations. You know, women used to not have that done unless they were pregnant.

SG: *Was that ignorance or modesty?* **CLC:** It was ignorant modesty! You just didn't go to the doctor except if something was serious. **SH:** Not just for a routine checkup. **CLC:** You went because you were hurting someplace. **SH:** And another thing is immunizations. As I understand it, the kids aren't being immunized now. But we look at our records every day because we fill out immunization records every day. And we did a good job of getting children immunized out here. And it wasn't a law then—of having children immunized. **CLC:** We were talking about that yesterday.

SG: *It was kind of shocking to hear that this country has the lowest immunization ratio.* **SH:** It's terrible. **CLC:** When we'd deliver one, that's the thing we'd try to keep up on. **SH:** When they came in for the six-week checkup, and most people would do that. **CLC:** Because it's free. **SH:** We always gave the baby its first immunizations at six weeks. Now, they may not come back for any more, but I imagine even that would help a little bit. But most people came back as they were supposed to. **CLC:** Before that, the health department would do it, but you've got to educate people. That's one of the biggest things. **SH:** It was not required for school. The only thing required by schools was the smallpox vaccination. Now you have to have all immunizations: whooping cough, diphtheria, tetanus, polio, measles, mumps, rubella.

SG: *Wait, how can Clinton say we have the lowest immunization record if you have to have them in order to go to school?* **SH:** Babies aren't getting them. Babies are getting measles. Babies should not have measles. Nobody should have measles. They should be immunized.

SG: *You mean, for some, the very first immunizations they get is when they go to school?* **SH:** Yes, they go to the health department. They can't go to school without them, and they won't.

SG: *And you still keep your records?* **SH:** Oh, we have all of our records.

SG: *You must have them housed in a building somewhere.* **CLC:** No, we've just got our house in a holy mess with records. **SH:** But they're not in the mess that she says. They really are not. We can put our hands on any record.

SG: *Of anyone you've ever seen?* **SH:** Yes, from 1948.

SG: *By the way, is it true that when you opened your office at first, Eldon Evans said that he was going down the street and looked up and you two were hanging out the window and he asked what you were doing and you said you were looking for patients?* **SH:** [Laughs] Probably did. Well, we may have said that, but that way it couldn't have been, because we didn't have that front office. But we were looking for patients. That didn't last long. Well, we could have been looking out the window and said that jokingly. But when we were looking for patients it was not from the front part of that office. Louise's dad had his law office there. We were back farther in that office. We didn't acquire that [the front] until later.

SG: *When you decided to move, was that a necessity?* **CLC:** Yes, it was a necessity. **SH:** Really, we were wasting too much time, even though we enjoyed going out on the deliveries. You know you have to wait, you have to wait awhile . . . and wait. **CLC:** I guess you could be there the whole day. And we have been. We most always told somebody where we were.

SG: *So you lived in the office and that way you could get some rest and still be with the patient? Were there any laws or rules about doing that?* **CLC:** The only thing was, you couldn't have the air conditioner going in the delivery room. **SH:** That's right, that was the law. We could not have it going in the delivery room because, well, we would give chloroform sometimes, and it would go all through the building. **CLC:** We didn't do much ether.

SG: *What would you use for childbirth?* **SH:** Chloroform or . . . **CLC:** Or we'd use Demerol.

SG: *Was that a matter of course, or did they ask?* **CLC:** Guess if they made enough noise you knew they needed something. **SH:** Lamaze and natural childbirth, that came later. We did a lot of Lamaze. Molly Carew taught the classes.

SG: *Is there a difference, I mean, a better, healthier baby without anesthetic?* **SH:** Well, your baby won't be sleepy and you don't run the chance of—well, a sleepy baby is not what you want. See, the baby gets the same anesthesia as the mother. It doesn't breathe as well, usually. Yes, it can impair the brain. If they don't breathe, it does. We didn't really give that much, but we gave chloroform with contractions toward the very end. We didn't give it really but at the very end.

SG: *Did you let fathers in the birthing room as they do now?* **SH:** Well, when we delivered at home, everybody was there. **CLC:** We had, I never will forget, in my office one time, we had a father in there and I was waiting for the baby to drain, had the head hanging out, and I guess he thought I was going to let it hang there and he tried to get over my shoulder. He thought I couldn't pull it out. **SH:** And that's a normal thing you do when the baby's head comes out. You wait and let it drain—mucus out.

SG: *Does it come out up or down?* **SH:** Down. **CLC:** When it's in the proper position. Yes, and just let it hang there a minute until [the mucus] runs out. The babies are pretty strong themselves. I think it's a miracle. I think every delivery is a miracle. I really do. They are almost able to take care of themselves from the word go. If they could just reach that bottle, they'd be all right.

SG: *Sometimes don't you think that children survive in spite of their parents?* **SH:** Oh, yes. Indeed. **CLC:** What did we see on TV about kids putting stuff in their mouth? **SH:** I think it was a commercial, but that is so true. **CLC:** Oh, it was a potato chip. Everything else they'd put in their mouth but not the wrong kind of potato chip.

SG: *I guess you've known them to swallow funny things.* **SH:** We had one kid that swallowed a silver dollar. In fact, do you know what? It was Tick's nephew. **CLC:** We've had a lot of 'em swallow money. **SH:** But this was a great big one. And we took a picture and there it was. It was huge, but it went through. A great big thing like that. This kid must have been, oh, he was big enough for it to come out. It was just beyond his throat. And so he just kept swallowing, and he knew immediately when it moved. He was so happy.

SG: *Was that the strangest thing?* **SH:** Oh, false teeth. Remember the man who couldn't find his false teeth? Well, they were in his throat. We just stuck a finger down there and got them out. Well, he'd had a stroke. His sister looked everywhere, and she couldn't find them, and she knew he couldn't possibly swallow them, and we looked, too. Of course, this happened the day before, and of course he wouldn't eat. So Louise stuck her finger down (see, this was at home) in his throat and there they were, and she got those teeth out. I don't know how in the world she did it because they were sideways down in his throat. **CLC:** I don't know, they looked like a big "C" or something. That was like turning a breech baby. Now with most babies there are no problems. In fact, you think you have a lot more problems than you do. **SH:**

If you'd just wait, most of the problems will take care of themselves. CLC: Just time is the answer many, many times.

SG: *Probably just having somebody there is the help.* SH: Oh, that means so much, it sure does. CLC: Yes, I've known my mother to go lots of places to be with that baby. I guess you'd go to help. I remember, with her friends, my momma would go to hold her hand or rub her head. My grandmother had fifteen children! Well, my grandfather came in one day when she had just had the fourth and fifth [twins] and he'd been up trying to "grub." Do you know what that is? That's to take the little bushes and trees and things off to clear a little piece of land so you can grow stuff. Well, he'd been working all day and he looked in, came in and put his hoe against the house and came in to talk to Granny. He said, "Oh, I don't see how I'll ever take care of these children." Well, they tell the tale that Granny sat up in the middle of the bed and said, "Abel Caudill, I can take care of these five children and myself, so surely to the Lord you can take care of yourself!" I think that's a true story, isn't it? SH: I've always heard it. CLC: So she went on and had ten more. They had been married three years and she had five children. Two sets of twins. The first ones were twins.

SG: *Were women tougher or healthier? Now we might have better food, and we don't work so hard.* CLC: Hard work is good for you. Now, I don't know, but I think a lot of them died early. Now, Granny's kids, every one of them grew to adults. SH: Young children would die. Just a certain number would die.

SG: *How old was your grandmother? How long did she live?* CLC: Oh, she was up there. Seventy or eighty. I didn't remember her very well, but she lived longer than my grandfather.

SG: *To change this a bit, Louise, what keeps you going?* CLC: Susie.

SG: *You met when? 1942?* SH: 1948. You graduated in 1947. No, 1946, because you went to Philadelphia. CLC: And I was up there a year and a half, and then I went over to Oneida. That's where I met Susie. Forty-five years, that's a long time. Not many people can get along for that many years.

SG: *More than get along—all day, working together. I imagine you went through a lot of hell together. I mean, tired and overworked, hungry. Just traveling with somebody is hard, but you are working under difficult circumstances. How did you do it?* SH: Well, we did different things. CLC: We never did fuss much. We were just lucky. SH: We both had the same ideas. I mean, when we first started out, we both intended to make medicine count for something. We really did. And we felt that way before we met each other. Definitely.

SG: *So how did you discover that you had the same goals? Discussion? Accident?* SH: Accident. CLC: I'm a great believer that most of the things that happen in this world are by accident. Call it anything you want to. But, to me, intellectually figuring it out very seldom works.

SG: *But you have to be smart enough to know which accidents are right. I think artists call them happy accidents.* SH: There, we worked hard. We worked really hard. CLC: The only thing to say was can you get a little sleep tonight. And it was night and day when we got started. That first month or so we were upset because we weren't working. SH: That did *not* last long. CLC: But, you see, we had so much to do and went out to deliver babies and carried all that junk to deliver 'em and then we had to come back home and get those things clean. Well, it might be three o'clock in the morning and we'd go over to Jane's house and put 'em in the washing machine. SH: That was when people had just started to have automatic washers. So we used Jane's whenever we came back from a delivery.

SG: *Did she leave the door open for you?* SH: Oh, everyone left their doors open. It was in the basement. We had to put them in right away and—oh, we were kept busy. CLC: And I hate to tell you, but Susie did most all the work. I was always sort of hanging back doing something else and that didn't make the work get better. SH: Well, but you had to study and do those things. CLC: Yes, I read a lot more than she did. SH: She had to, you know. I mean, she had to figure out something when [she] {you} hadn't had the experience before. And we felt we had to do whatever it was—whatever was presented to try to take care of it. We sent people to Lexington, but it took a long time then to go to Lexington. But other than X-ray and doing blood count, which we did—I mean, I took blood counts because Louise taught me how because she still knew how. CLC: Oh, I'll never forget trying to do a spinal tap on a baby on my knee. Now, I wouldn't do a spinal tap today for nothing. I had this little kid, and we wondered if it had meningitis, and you could tell pretty well by a spinal tap. So I just took an ordinary little needle and it worked just great. Now I wouldn't do that—no way. SH: No way.

SG: *Because you know what could happen.* CLC: Because you got other people who can do it. We've got the facilities. We didn't have any place back then. You did it where you were.

SG: *Now, would you say that either one of you could have accomplished your ideas or dedication without the other?* SH: It never occurred to me to think about it. CLC: No. I'll never forget I went to get Susie out of a show one afternoon because we had to go deliver a baby and I was afraid to go by myself. Susie was on a date. **SH:** Yes, I was on a date at a movie, and Louise came in and got me. I remember that, yes.

SG: *What about the date?* **SH:** I think maybe he came with us.

SG: *It's wonderful to see the admiration you have for each other. Has that seemed to grow over the years?* **SH:** Oh, yes.

SG: *I wonder—and you don't have to answer this—but Susie, you have worked with Louise all your life and then Louise has made honorary this and that . . .* **CLC:** No, it's not fair, it makes me feel . . . **SH:** It makes Louise feel bad. **CLC:** I don't like to get those things [awards]. **SH:** Oh, I'm the supporting actress.

SG: *They get Academy Awards, too. And it's no use being the lead in the play if the people around aren't really good.* **SH:** It makes Louise feel bad. It doesn't make me feel bad. **CLC:** It always makes me feel bad, and I can't understand why she doesn't get mad. I think I'd really get mad. **SH:** I really don't, and I don't have any deep-seated resentment, either. I don't. **CLC:** Well, it's just not fair. [Susie received an honorary doctorate from MSU in December 1996.]

SG: *That's why the title of the play is as it is. The title doesn't have your name on it—it has hers, "Me 'n Susie."* **CLC:** Well, that's the way it is except it's mostly Susie.

SG: *That sounds like a good last line, "It was me 'n Susie, but mostly Susie." But that's the way it is now, and you don't mind that? I did want to ask you if you thought I might interview your sister Lucille.* **CLC:** I think you'd have a better subject if you'd write on her.

SG: *Also, I talked with Mr. Evans and he told me this [if I can use it], and he said that you took care of his mother and that when Louise came to see her she would just get in bed with her—and then be telling Susie what to do. And I thought, how comforting for a patient.* **SH:** Well, what she would do was just get up on the bed, touching.

SG: *Do you know how rare that is today? Some doctors just write you a prescription but don't touch you unless they have to. Do you think that is important?* **CLC:** I think that's important. Nowadays it's a lot different. The whole philosophy of living is different today than it was thirty years ago. People think differently now. Now you'd be considered a screwball, or you'd be a gay, or you'd be—what is it they say about men—oh, abusive. I mean, you know, they make something out of everything nowadays. **SH:** Now, a male doctor especially has to be very careful. If he pats that little lady on the arm, why . . . **CLC:** You could be sued for that. **SH:** And if he pats you on the butt, for sure he will.

SG: *If it has become so that you can't touch people anymore, aren't we*

taking away a lot of healing possibilities? **CLC**: I think so, yes. And
it's our custom, and I don't know how we ever got into such a mess.
But it seems like it's getting worse and worse. If we have a few more
government interferences. . . . Besides, a person's personal life is their
personal life.

SG: *Well, anyway, I was struck by what a personal comfort that must have
been. Maybe you can still do it.* **SH**: Oh, she still does. But we don't
make many house calls now. **CLC**: I know I most always take them
by the shoulders or always touch them. They usually are sitting there
in that chair and I'll open the door and go [tap on the shoulder] and
say, "How are you there? I haven't seen you for a while."

SG: *I'm sure it's natural for you. Maybe that is a part of the healing right
there.* **CLC**: It really is.

SG: *So, if no one touches you, you can just curl up and die?* **CLC**: You
can just curl up and die. It wouldn't be a very pleasant way to do it.
But a lot of people want to do it. I mean, people want to die.

SG: *I thought people fought right up to the last.* **CLC**: I don't think so.
Oh, some do, don't get me wrong, but now you see how many people
write a living will—don't do this and don't do that. **SH**: But that doesn't
mean they want to die. That means they don't want to be bothered if
they are going to die. **CLC**: But who knows when they are going to
die? **SH**: Well, you know if you're not breathing, you're not living and
you don't want to be on a respirator.

SG: *Are you saying that this shouldn't happen?* **CLC**: I'm a great believer
that you should get rid of all the pain you can get rid of.

Dr. Claire Louise Caudill and Susie Halbleib making a house call in the early years of their practice. Photo by Art Stewart.

Dr. Louise and Susie with two sets of twins, about 1959. Photo by *Morehead News*.

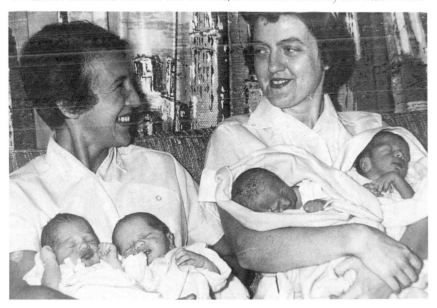

All photos are courtesy of Dr. Caudill unless otherwise indicated.

Mr. and Mrs. Daniel Boone Caudill and their family on the occasion of their fiftieth wedding anniversary, 1958. Louise stands behind her father.

The Caudill family home at 326 North Wilson Avenue, Morehead.

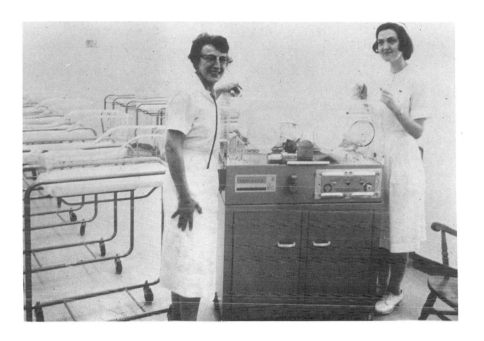

Dr. Louise and Susie at the Oneida Maternity Center, Clay County, in 1947.

Dr. Louise's medical office, built in 1957, at 310 Main Street, Morehead, Kentucky, where she still practices.

The first section of the St. Claire Medical Center, built in 1963. Courtesy of St. Claire Medical Center.

The original Sisters of Notre Dame as they appeared in 1963, when St. Claire Medical Center opened. Left to right, Sisters Mary Rita Claire, Mary Louise, Mary Jean Ann, Mary Thomasina, and Jeanne Frances. Courtesy of St. Claire Medical Center.

Dr. Louise (in white at right) and the Sisters of Notre Dame examining plans for the first addition to the St. Claire Medical Center. Mother Joelle, now the Mother General in Rome, is seen at right of Dr. Louise. Courtesy of St. Claire Medical Center.

Susie's room in Dr. Louise's office, with photos of many of her "babies," children she and Susie delivered.

Dr. Louise using bunny to demonstrate for play director Dr. Travis Preston
Lockhart how to do a breech delivery.

Sister Jeanne Frances with baby
Deveney Redwine in 1996. Sister
Jeanne was one of the original
Sisters and is still on the staff of the
hospital. Courtesy of St. Claire
Medical Center.

In 1995 Dr. Louise was named "Country Doctor of the Year" by the Country Doctor Museum in Bailey, North Carolina, and Staff Care, Inc., and her story was written up nationwide. Photo courtesy of *USA Today*.

Dr. Louise after receiving an honorary doctorate from the University of Louisville School of Medicine in 1996. At left is Dr. Don Kmetz, dean of the School of Medicine; at right, John Schumaker, president of the University of Louisville.

Curtain call at the premiere performance of "Me 'n Susie," November 12, 1993, at Morehead State University. Left to right, Susie Halbleib, Shirley Gish, Dr. Louise, and Elizabeth Victor, who portrayed the young Louise in the first performance. Photo by Eric Shindlebauer, courtesy of Morehead State University.

Susie Halbleib and Shirley Gish at the "Me 'n Susie" party following the performance of the play. Photo by Eric Shindlebauer, courtesy of Morehead State University.

Lucille Caudill Little
May 29, 1993

Lucille Caudill Little is Louise's elder sister. Born in Morehead on August 20, 1909, she was married to W. Paul Little (September 27, 1907 October 28, 1990) and lives in Lexington, Kentucky. Like Louise, she has a sense of social consciousness and charm and charisma, yet these close sisters are very different. From the interviews, it is evident that they were different even as children and took far different paths. Lucille was an actress, singer, and theater founder. She is now a patron of the arts whose generosity and support have already made lasting marks on the culture of this area.

Well, Louise and I are used to being called by the wrong name. I used to be called Louise and she was called Lucille. She was really supposed to be called Claire and I was supposed to be Mary. Because we had a Mary Ann and Mary Angela for grandmothers. Both grandmothers, so I got that name and she got Claire from an aunt in Oklahoma, and where did Louise come from?

I was the oldest and then came Louise and then Boone, Jane's husband, and then they skipped six years. There were three years between each of us and then there were six years between Boone and Bud and three between Bud and Patty.

There was theatre here in Morehead early, when I was growing up, and the first thing I remember is we had the Chautauqua here. And you know, that was quality theatre. We had it every summer.

There was a school started here in Morehead by Frank Button. Now he was the only male graduate of Midway College at that time, and that's very interesting. One of the teachers that we had up here, almost at the very beginning—until she died—was Miss Inez Faith Humphries. She came from up in Illinois and she wanted to be a missionary and they wouldn't accept her because she was a little wiry woman and they didn't think her health—oh, yes, and her eyes were bad—so she was a teacher always. So she came here to help with the school at Midway—they called it Midway Orphan Girls' School. It was for orphan girls when it began. They needed teachers, so, well, Frank Button's mother was from the same place Miss Humphries was from. From out in Illinois. And they solicited her to teach at Midway. She was a recent widow and had this young son and she said she'd come there "only if my son can go to school there." And he really is the only male graduate. There's a lot of history here.

But anyway, General Withers financed Frank Button's coming here and starting the school mainly because there had been feuds and all the goings on in Rowan County and to try to clean the place up, and that was pretty early on. It was sort of like a school beyond high school, a normal school, sort of teachers' training. You could get a high school degree and graduate with that or go on and get another degree and become a teacher. Both Mother and Dad graduated from this normal school. I think Dad was five years ahead of Mother.

Anyway, what I'm trying to show you is that early on there was a lot of cultural promotion in this area, even from outside. People coming in. And it caught on. You know, really, it's just like every Sunday after church we went down to see the train pull in. Well, the train was kind of new and reached out, you know, to the world. Everybody wanted to reach out.

Really, the telephone office had been one of our big sources of information. Oh, the telephone office! All you had to do was pick up the phone and say, "Can you tell me where Dad is?" [Laughs.] Oh, that's the truth. It functioned right down to the center of Main Street. Oh, the operator could tell you anything—just could tell you anything that was going on.

Grandmother and Grandfather Caudill had five children in three years: a set of twins, a single, and then another set of twins. I think Grandfather was scared to death, but Grandmother told him off. "You just tend to all of these things you got going, and I'll just tend to the children." So after that, they had ten more. Ten boys and five girls and they all kind of taught each other. Every single one of them lived to adulthood. Every single one of them had good health, and every single one of them lived a genteel, good life; got in no trouble. It's really remarkable when you stop to think of fifteen of them.

And I can say this, too. Our family was very democratic. We have a history of democratic action in the family. Dad really believed in it, and his family, when they made decisions, they all got together and they voted, just like you do in your government. Dad did that with us, too. His brothers, the two oldest twins [were] redheaded as fire. Why, both sets of the twins were. They were just copper heads. And those identical twins married identical twins, two redheaded women. And each of those couples had four redheaded children. Figure that one out.

But Louise never was redheaded. When she came back from internship, everyone said, oh, Louise had dyed her hair. And Louise is kind of the last one you'd expect to. Her hair had always been chestnut, but when she came back from interning, her hair was black, black just like Mother's. You see, she hadn't been able to be out in the sun and carry on with tennis and all her other things. All her life her hair had been sunburned, and so we thought she was chestnut haired.

I was a redhead. And then, on Mother's side, Mother's grandmother was real redheaded. Ophelia Talliafero—or Tolliver—as they came to be known, but they were originally Talliafero. Now, some of them still call it Talliafero, and there's quite a genealogical study done on them by our cousin John in New York. His sister is a genealogist, and she has followed that through. And the old house, that would have been Great-grandmother Tolliver's husband's father's home. Well, that would be interesting to follow because, you know, they were all shooting and drinking. All of the Tollivers were.

You know, Louise and I stood in the window and saw the last of them—I guess it was our Great-uncle Cate—saw him shot to death. Oh, we were real young. I mean, here was Dad in the window, and we were just barely neck over the windowsill in the old courthouse. Well, sure, everybody already knew there was trouble outside. See, Cate came into town drunk, I guess, and, you see, it was all politics, power struggle, just like it is today, the same blessed problems. You know, I think it's almost worse today than it was then. But, anyway, the Martins had stolen the election—or so the Tollivers thought. But it was all, you know, it just went on and on and on, and the families never gave up hating each other. It's just like today and it's just like what Dad went through, but it was power politics and alcohol and guns. But there wasn't that much money floating around, but the main thing was to have your gun on your hip and your bottle on the other hip, I guess.

We weren't scared to go out on the streets. Oh, no, this was just a very dramatic, different sort of thing. It wasn't something that happened every day. Oh, no, I wasn't nearly as afraid as I am right now today in Lexington. But, of course, I'm really not afraid. But today there is really more ugliness that goes on for women, more abuse, in my mind, than there was then for men. Women were treated better then. It was mainly for power.

Oh, we just had a good time, growing up here in Morehead. At first we lived down in the center of town. We'd have lemonade stands. We'd have that whenever Court Day came. Then the Evanses had a big family, and they were two doors down, and they'd come over, and because I was the oldest I'd have to make all the candy. They'd stir it, though. Oh, and angel food cakes. I bet I've made enough angel food cakes. . . . We'd all do it together. There were always things going on, but the real developing culture here was from the church and the school. School here was always good, and it was quality. I even had drama lessons. You know, they called it "elocution." And I had private music lessons, both voice and piano. We had folk dancing. We had all of this as kids.

Oh, and little plays. I can remember, every time it rained I'd go up into those hills back of the house. I had my little secret house up there which was raked off, you know, cleaned up, and it was where there was a wonderful growth of trailing arbutus and Indian Pipes. [I] can remember those two. And close was a beautiful peach-colored mountain laurel. And when Mother found out, she didn't much care for me going up there in the rain. Why, I'd go up there and sing and act. And I'd be all by myself, and I could scream, you know, as loud as I wanted to and nobody knew. I tried my voice out. Oh, I'll never forget those days.

I can still remember Miss Evelyn Royalty, who was the drama teacher at the normal school, and I would go and watch her rehearsals all the time. I was too little to be in the plays, but Marie Holbrook—oh, I can remember the part she played—I'd go home and say her lines . . . and I remember the porch, the upstairs porch on our house. I'd go up there and speak out to all the town. I always knew then that I wanted to sing and act.

And here is one advantage that I really had. Mary Sue Miller played the piano—just made it up, she was wonderful—at the movies. So if the horses were running, she could make the piano sound like that, or sweet sounds of romance or whatever at the movie house. It was right where Battson's Drugstore is now. That old building was built of brick-sized stone, and that's where the movie was. And she would say that I had to go with her and turn the pages, but she never used pages! [Laughs.] So I didn't have to pay, and it might have been a nickel, but I always got to go to the movies, and it was just a few doors from our home. And I saw movie after movie after movie, but I don't remember any of the actors now.

But they were without voices, you see, without sound, and Mary Sue, playing this piano all the way through. And you had to read captions and she played what was going on. Well, I would say that that and Miss Royalty's rehearsals—well, I'd come home and try to do them. And I had the pleasure of studying with Miss Royalty, too. She was as great as anyone I ever had. And then, when I went to boarding school [Hamilton College, Lexington], I had a fabulous trainer, Miss Julia Connelly. And at the same time I went there, I had private lessons in everything. Oh, I can remember Dad saying once, "Well, I said that whatever it costs me to send Lucille to go to school, I would have to set enough aside for those that followed her." Then he said, "I don't know whether I can or not. I didn't know that with Lucille how expensive it gets." And so the first twenty-five dollars that I ever made singing, I mailed it to him, and he framed it! And I'd like to see that. I'd love to see that. I do know he framed that check.

But he never said I couldn't do it. Oh, no. But I learned, early on, to try to get those scholarships or fellowships, and the first big one I got was at Ohio State. It was in music. And one of the greatest teachers I ever had was in Florida at Stetson. Paul Geddes of the Geddes family. His brother designed and executed the whole set for Oberammergau. Barbara Bel Geddes was his niece, and her father was Norman Bel Geddes. He was a teacher I had. He was going blind, but he was great. And he had a ladder that you reached up and climbed to develop the diaphragm. This was something that I learned early on. The fact is, I would say, that Miss Royalty had us do exercises for the diaphragm, but I learned voice production singing in the hills or on the top porch.

I'd try to teach Louise and my husband things like Christmas carols or "My Old Kentucky Home," and I never could teach either one of them. But you just let them listen to me sing, they could critique me better than anyone! Oh, yes, because I would take anything they'd say, you know, for my own good. But I can remember both of them telling me I made too big faces, you know, singing. But you have to make faces with your mouth so far open. I overdid it possibly, and I sure heard the good criticism they made of me. It stayed stuck up here. Don't overdo.

We played together as kids, except, if anything happened wrong, Mother blamed me and I got my legs switched. I was never free of Louise and Boone. I was always responsible for them. And if I tried—well, I can remember this happening, right where you come down from Wilson Avenue at Main Street. We had one or two cars in town then. And here came a car, and I wasn't used to a car, and I ran across the street, and I made it. But, boy, the car had to screech and throw on the brakes and twist around to miss Louise. Well, everybody in town told Mother. So I got my legs switched. She generally sent you out for your own switch. I think Mother did that to discipline me. You bet she did. She'd discipline anyone around her. Even Daddy. You had to go get your own switch. Oh, and she told how big to get it. And it better not break. About this big, one that would whip, one that won't break. It couldn't be a twig.

But Louise was doing circuses. Oh, listen, we all were in it, of course. But I didn't have anything to do with all those snakes and worms and things they got. And see, I couldn't stand that, but Louise loved all that.

I was the one who liked to be dressed up pretty—oh, always. But Mother did that, and I would wear green and Louise would wear yellow. I would wear blue and she would wear pink dresses. They would be made alike. I don't think we minded that too much. I don't think we ever looked too much alike.

We had a good childhood. We had a happy family. It was a great time.

My parents were happy together. They loved each other. Mother got to pretty much rule the roost at home, and Dad ruled wherever he was outside the home. And they were like Mutt and Jeff. Mother was shorter than you, Louise, and then you and Pat and then me—that was the way our heights went. But Mother had these wonderful big blue eyes and this white, white skin—whiter than the driven snow. And this black hair. And Daddy used to always say, "Well, I've got three mighty pretty girls, but not a one of them can live up to their mother."

And we played games all the time. Like Louise said, we played hard and we studied hard and we worked hard. On Saturdays we'd all be out cleaning cars and here would come Frances, our housekeeper/cook, bringing out a great big chocolate cake and two gallons of milk. And we'd stop all our work and eat that whole darn cake. Then she'd go in, you see, because we were getting ready to go to camp, and she fixed all this food for us to take to the river. And she'd go in and bake another cake. And we still like chocolate cake. But we really had a good time, do you see? We really, honestly did.

And Louise—now, I was never as athletic as the rest—but Louise came along and they all did acrobatics. I can remember, as a child, our grandparents on our mother's side had the hotel down on Main Street. Great big old building. When I was little bitty we didn't have bathtubs in the house. We had one on Main Street, but we had to carry water in there. And we stewed and sputtered about it. But Louise would climb up the facings of doors, you know, hands and feet on each side. And she would teach all the rest of us to do that and flips and just all kinds of athletics. Dad really motivated all our athletic activity.

And then Uncle Bert had a movie house right next door in the hotel, and we'd get to sell the tickets and go to the movie. Then Uncle Herb had a soda fountain on down the street and the best chocolates. I can't remember what kind, but they were blue ribbon. And he would go off on a date on Sundays, and he'd let me run—and Louise did it, too—that soda fountain. Our friends would come in and, boy, the banana splits, you know, and everything in the world. We'd heap them up. And they loved to come in when we were running it. And we ate all the candy we wanted. They made their own ice cream then with big paddles—about that long and that big around—and those things would shake back and forth somehow and freeze that cream. And then it was made out of cream and milk and eggs. All good stuff.

Oh, and I'll tell you an experience I had that was wonderful for me. Now, the Millers [they ran the freight depot] had about six girls and one boy. And Nell, the oldest one, married Bill Young. Nell taught piano and

I took piano from her. Well, they lived where the Evanses lived later, but Bill Young built that. (He was a brother to Allie Young.) Nell married Bill Young. He bought her a grand piano, and the Millers were just about all musical. So I took piano lessons from Nell Miller Young. And in the summer, when I was about eleven maybe, she would go up to the Cincinnati Conservatory and study and teach in the summer. And Mother would let me go with her. And so I had that wonderful experience of going up there. I don't know how many summers. Three, I'd say, anyway. Maybe more.

And I studied with Dan Beddoe, who was one of the outstanding voice teachers, and Maybel Blockson, who was in children's theatre. So two things I was always interested in in my life, I got very early up there. I had a wonderful time and, you know, so young, it was great experience. Mother only let me go because she trusted Nell, and Nell took care of me, and living in the big city and riding streetcars to town—oh, that was all quite an experience. I'd guess by that time there were a few more cars here in Morehead. Our uncles had one of the first cars.

My first performance singing, of course, it was at church. Solos, sure. And it was nice I had that opportunity. Then I went to Ohio State. I got a fellowship in voice. It was the first they had ever offered. And Major Wall and Dr. Hughes were head of the music department. And I had wonderful opportunities up there. I'd had the same opportunities at Hamilton while I was there. I was soloist with the Transylvania Glee Club. And they traveled all over and that was a great experience.

At Transylvania I traveled and then when I went to Stetson in Florida for Paul Geddes, I was the soloist. They had a symphony orchestra and they had a chorus. It was a Baptist school. And Dr. Hulley Howard, he was the president at Stetson, he went out and preached at some church every Sunday and I'd have to go and sing with him. And I would always go and sing in a church the Sunday before we would have a recital there. I think they took up a collection. I don't think they ever charged them for us to come. But that was wonderful experience. I had solo experience.

I did lots of acting. I really think I prefer directing. I started out the Studio Players in Lexington. And I did their first two plays. Off and on I did plays for them, and then, before that, we had organized children's theatre through the recent graduates of the American Association of University Women. I worked hard with children's theatre always. It was really set up to be for children by children.

Then came a paid director, and it changed the whole format of what we were doing. We were having children come backstage and help with makeup, with costumes, with the whole technical business as well as act and usher and, you know, I've always said that the theatre was an all-consuming effort. You've got to have music, you've got to have dance, you've got painters and carpenters. . . . Absolutely anything you want to do you can kind of place it in the theatre, and that's why I loved it. Because you get all people together to do something cooperatively and so you can appreciate it. I've been sold on it as an educational process. I think that it develops creativity. I've been quoted saying something that—I don't know if it is very smart or not—that I don't think you are educated until you become creative. And I do believe that.

I think the good teacher, I don't care what she's teaching, develops creativity and makes them imagine and dream up things and makes life and makes situations, work them out. I really think that. You have to give them that chance. That's exactly the way I feel. Some didn't agree with me and said, "Oh, you can't get every child to act." I said, "Oh, I think so." I've never seen a child that couldn't go off and be doing something by themselves. I've never seen one. Make-believe is natural.

For example, a funny thing happened. We were in Israel, I believe. The bus broke down, and another little bus was broken down right next to us, and it was full of little kids. So, here were all these little kids running around. They had been at a camp of Palestinians and just suddenly, when our bus broke down, and here all these children descended upon us. And then they had to repair the tires. We were all in Israeli territory. And so, just to amuse the children, we started playing like we were the bus. We all wound up pretending we were a bus and then we broke down, and we pretended to repair.

But, about Louise, you want to know what makes people love Louise so much? What appeal does she have? Her creativity. That's it exactly. You see, I have said that what I want to do with the worldly goods I have is to give it to education, mainly through the arts, to develop creativity. Well, through the arts, I say, because that's been *my* interest. And then I have to stop and think, but my sister is all in science, and if it were not for her creativity, I don't think she would have had the power or been the excellent health promoter. I mean, she has promoted health in this area through understanding people and her creative attitude with her understanding of them. Weezer thinks she's not, but I know that she is more creative than anyone could ever dream.

We were taught that. We grew up that way, but we grew up with rules. I wouldn't say that they were written down, but we followed the pattern of our parents, do you see? And we were taught—do what you want to do. However, Dad wanted me to be a lawyer, and I got a fellowship in music, and I went on doing what I wanted to do. He wanted Louise to be a lawyer, and Louise balked. She always wanted to go to med school, so she went.

Boone, to tell you the truth, was a musician, probably just with his whole being, and the first boy. Then Dad wanted him to become a lawyer. Now, Dad didn't realize he was doing this to us. But he did. He wanted someone in his office with him and doing his thing with him and sharing all of the things he liked. So Boone got through law school. He responded to Dad's wanting us to be in his image. Oh, it wasn't so much his wanting us to be in his image as he wanted our company.

Daddy, he just loved us so that he wanted us there working with him and doing his thing, where he could see us every day and be proud of us. I think that was it. He just wanted us with him. When I was real young and Louise came along, Mother would send me off with Dad wherever he went. And I'd be dressed up and Dad would be proud of me. He'd take my hand, and if he were going to a committee meeting in Lexington, I'd go with him. I was always respectful.

I can remember when they built the road from here, I guess, to Mt. Sterling in 1960. He was the county chairman or something like that. He would have to go to Lexington for meetings, and he'd take me with him. And then when his older twin brothers bought some land in Shelbyville, I went with him. He would go down there to make all the arrangements. I would go with him because it would give Mother relief, and Boone was there then. So, to begin with, I was a little more with Dad and they were a little more with Mother because of necessity, I guess.

I started the drama and speech department at Morehead State University. Well, Miss Royalty did something good for me, and Miss Connelly, too. So then you pass it on, that's right. Then I think I got more into directing when I studied with Milton Smith at Columbia. And then to have had that and to have studied voice, too, was an amazing thing to me. But I had two teachers at the same time that taught me the symbolism, the importance of color. Color has been a directive of my whole life.

So what color would I use for Louise? Well, you would have to put some yellow and there would have to be some depth, some earthy something. And spiritual. Well, you see, Louise's whole life is lifted up. I mean, you would have a lot of vertical lines in her life that are really firmly grounded and spread out, like a tree. The people that she has touched in life and how it has all been from the trunk, which is the basic *her*—and the creative thing and how she's reached all these lives. And that is kind of like a tree. I would do Louise kind of like a tree.

Dr. Claire Louise Caudill and Susie Halbleib
March 27, 1993

By this time I felt ready for questions that were beyond the factual or chronological. I began to try to visualize Dr. Louise on the stage speaking to people, speaking to people's hearts and souls as she does to individual patients. What would she say to young people? Did she have advice? How do you tap into another person's wisdom? Her response to my opening question was completely spontaneous—and quite remarkable.

SG: *If you could sit down in a room full of fifteen- and sixteen-year-old high school girls from eastern Kentucky who want to know you, have advice from you, what would you like to say?* **CLC:** If you think it could be a difference between a better life for somebody—for these young women. Maybe they were never encouraged by anybody. Maybe no one ever told them they could do anything. . . . Maybe what you say is going to make a difference. I think of those things. Hmmm. Well, I think there are a few things that are important. I think that you can do anything you want to do, if it's real and if you really want to do it. You can do it. I do believe women have a harder time than men. I believe the problem is just not that simple. But I believe you can do it, and I think you can make your way. Now, how do you do it?

I think you have to keep a goal as you go along—in your mind. Then, well, you just look out there and see the stars and you want one. . . . Well, you don't get it that way. I believe you have to be capable and you have to train yourself. I think you have to be physically able. You have to socially be able to adjust to people and you have to listen to those daggone emotions. I'm a great believer that affect is a great deal more important than intelligence. That's a lot of words to say, guess, but I really believe that. You have to have the "feel" of things more than anything else. And I believe that is a big part of health. I believe that a healthy body is particularly influenced by your feelings, whether they are the feelings for your religion, or your adjustment to society, or your social status, or your cultural level. I don't know, but I think that that's what makes you *you*. It's the soul. It's the spirit.

And everybody can do it. Everybody out here has something that you desire to do. Just try to evaluate it and see how you fit into the picture. I don't think you can take anybody and try to copy them. I think you have to make your situation fit with you. I can't wear those fancy hats and those high-heeled shoes. That's not me. That's somebody quite foreign as far as I'm concerned. I like to sort of be prissed up, but I don't like all that fancy junk. Everybody has to figure it out for themselves.

My daddy always said you could do whatever you wanted to do. My mother believed you had to look fancy and do things that were fitting. I got a little bit from both sides. I studied. I wasn't smart. I believe you don't have to be smart. I believe if you work hard enough you can make up for your ignorance. And I don't believe that 'cause I was from eastern Kentucky that I was any more ignorant than they are in Lexington or Louisville or anyplace else. I don't think that where you are from is any measure of intelligence. I don't think just 'cause you aren't from something that you aren't smart either.

I really believe you can do it, I mean, if you want it. But you have to have a stimulus from someplace. But I believe you can pull it from within. The influence from the outside helps too . . . (Oh, dear, I was hardly ready for this.)

Now, I sort of believe that people are basically good. I believe that, basically, everybody is made good. And it's a great satisfaction to feel like you've done something that's worthwhile. I mean that, within yourself, it sort of makes you feel like your life hasn't been a waste. I don't care what you do, if you do it well and enjoy doing it. Oh, I feel like I'm preaching a sermon. [Laughs.] I'm not very good at sermons.

SG: *Sounds more like encouragement. And what about health? What would you tell these young women about taking care of themselves?*
CLC: Well, I think that just like you take care of your mind, you take care of your body. The physical part of it is important. Physically, you just have to obey the basic laws. Eat right, sleep right, don't drink too much, don't smoke, and don't play around when you shouldn't be playing around! Try to do the things that you feel within yourself are right. If you feel like it's right, it more than likely is.

SG: *What about peer pressure? I mean, the rate of teenage pregnancy in this area is high.* CLC: Well, that rate is high everywhere. I mean, this teen sex thing has gone crazy. That is the greatest pressure on a young person today and I think that, well, I was just reading some stuff here. I think the amount of children that have had intercourse from the ages of fifteen to seventeen in the past few years [the last twenty years] has gone from about 15 to 70 percent! So I think that's the attitude of the day.

SG: *You'd think that people were getting brighter, would know more or know the consequences, and that it would go down. How do you talk to these young girls, thirteen and fourteen? How do you talk to them?*
CLC: You can't talk to them. If they have that attitude at twelve or thirteen, I don't think you can change their mind. I think you have to begin before they fall in love. I think somebody else—the parent, the doctor—can help. You can be a friend to them. It's very difficult. I've seen lots of young girls get pregnant. I try to talk to them. In fact, I try to get them on birth control pills. I say, if you want to have intercourse, you ought to be protected. Not that I think that all girls ought to do that, but I think that if they are going to have intercourse, they better be protected.
SG: *What is the youngest mother you've ever had?* **CLC:** Oh, I imagine thirteen or fourteen. Thirteen. **SH:** Yes, she was twelve when she got pregnant.
SG: *Are women the weaker ones?* **CLC:** I don't think we are weaker. Only physically. **SH:** Oh, yes, they are. Women are. **CLC:** I mean, physically we aren't made that way. Why, our legs bow out, our arms bow out. A man is made in a straight line. Men are made physically stronger, but I don't think that means that they are stronger in any other fashion.
SG: *Do you think that life for eastern Kentucky women has changed any or improved?* **CLC:** It has become more like the rest of the world. Now, whether that's an improvement or not, I'm not entirely sure. [Laughs.] I guess they decided they needed the outside world, and I think that that part of it is right.
SG: *Why do you suppose people come to you and ask you questions like this?* **CLC:** I don't know. Ask Susie.
SG: *Susie, how would you answer that same question? This group of girls wants your advice.* **SH:** I think it is important for young women to learn to do something to take care of themselves. I really do. I think that's awfully important. I mean, I think that having a family and having a home life—I think it's great for young women to stay at home. It's good for the children; it's good for the mother. But I still think she has to keep in touch with the outside world and not be totally dependent on her husband. We are all independent. . . . I think, well, first of all, that a lot about sex needs to be taught in the home, and I think parents have that responsibility to teach their children about sex and about lots of things. And, no, not that it's bad but that you don't have to have sex before it's time. And you need to know the responsibilities, such as having a baby and diseases, and some of them learn, they do. But I think

women can do anything they want to do. They may not be able to dig ditches as far down as some man, but other than that, women can do anything. There's not a doubt in my mind that women can, and should, do whatever they want, but I still think it is great for a young woman to stay home and take care of her babies if she can at all. In this day and age, a lot of women can't. I guess when you're pulled in two directions, you just have to do the best you can.

SG: *This next question may be a biggie, and maybe you can't or won't answer it. Today more and more people can't afford to take care of themselves. They can't afford health care. Is there an answer? Why has health care gotten into such a state, or has it always been like this?* SH: I don't think it's always been, do you? People not being able to take care of themselves. CLC: Well, I don't know. How many babies did we deliver for nothing?

SG: *I guess you can't say, "Well, sorry, don't birth that baby."* SH: But I guess there's always going to be people who can't afford it.

SG: *Is there any way out of this?* CLC: Oh, let the government take care of them? That's what they're tryin' for, isn't it?

SG: *But that looks like a lot more money going to a lot more administrators. Is there any other way? Maybe go back and start all over?* CLC: Might be the answer. We'll call you some morning at 3 a.m. and say, "Here's the answer."

SG: *If you've got the answer, you can call me then. Do you see people neglect their health because of cost? Not doing things they might have done?* CLC: I believe you can see that in mammograms as much as anything. It costs so much to have mammography that people say, "I just don't want to have that done." It's almost a daily thing.

SG: *So what other health advice can you give?* CLC: Yes, I think we've done real good now as far as rural water is concerned. A lot of places didn't have near as much as we did, and that makes a big difference.

SG: *You mean there were outhouses?* CLC: Well, we had one on Main Street.

SG: *There was no indoor plumbing?* CLC: No.

SG: *So, if you had to go in the middle of the night, you had to go to the outhouse?* CLC: Well, and you had a slop jar. Not much fun, either.

SG: *How'd you take a bath?* CLC: In a washtub. On the back porch or kitchen.

SG: *You said there were places with dirt floors. I imagine they weren't exactly taking bubble baths every day. Did that affect the babies at all?* SH: Well, they are babies. They get diarrhea if you do not breastfeed them. CLC: Yes, but I don't think there were any more anomalies. We really had very few. **SH:** Yes, and really the diet is not too bad. They ate a lot of beans, and they are very nutritious. Most people canned tomatoes. **CLC:** And they didn't take medicine. **SH:** That's true, too.

SG: *You mean that's good?* **CLC:** That's good.

SG: *So it's better for the child if there are no drugs in you?* **CLC:** Well, I think the mother develops certain immunities and things from where she lives, and the child comes right into that environment.

SG: *What would you say success is?* **CLC:** Success comes in lots of different forms, different kinds of packages, and is different for each person. Being able to do something and then doing it, I believe that's about as quick as I can say it. You just can't do your work if you don't enjoy it. I preach that sermon every now and then.

SG: *Would you say you were lucky, or did you know you were going to like it?* **CLC:** I was mostly lucky, but I had a fairly good idea of what I wanted to do. I didn't really think it was going to be as hard as it was.

SG: *As hard as it was? The studying or the actual practice?* **CLC:** Either one. Both.

SG: *What was the "hard" that you didn't expect?* **CLC:** Well, I thought I could comprehend better than I could. I wasn't as smart as I thought I was, from the studying viewpoint. From the working viewpoint, I just couldn't go all day long, and that was when I was a darn sight younger than I am now. It was just physically taxing. If I had one place I had to go to, I had to stop three times going up that hill—and that was from the very beginning. **SH:** We just had to go day and night and day and night. **CLC:** We had one place we used to go to, and I had to stop three times going up that hill, and that was from the very beginning. I just could not make it.

SG: *You mean you had to walk to places?* **CLC:** Oh, all the time. Oh, honey, we walked all the time. **SH:** Oh, we got our exercise in our younger days, let me tell you. We did! Oh, we walked a lot! Well, you know, you'd go as far as you could, but you can't take the car up a hill when there's no road. Oh, there were a lot of times we had to walk. **CLC:** We've gone out every way you could think of, except airplane.

SG: *Were you ever a doctor in this hospital, like, in the emergency ward?* **CLC:** For a little while we were, for a short period of time. Until, you know, we got somebody there. But I delivered babies in the hospital. **SH:** When I think of in the beginning, you admitted lots of them. I mean, she admitted a lot. **CLC:** Yes, I admitted the first patient. She had pneumonia, I think.

SG: *Did the hospital fill up right away?* **CLC:** We just had forty-two beds, and we didn't have much trouble filling it up.

SG: *How involved are you in this new addition?* **CLC:** Oh, I'm just on the board. We just have a plan. I think it is to open July 1994. I know they are on schedule.

SG: *Susie, we really got off somewhere on your advice.* **SH:** Yes, well, I think that nutrition is really important. **CLC:** And no smoking—she'll say that. **SH:** Yes, no smoking, that's important. But nutrition is big on my list.

SG: *What's your idea of nutrition?* **SH:** Nutrition? Oh, eating, just like the book says, eating grains, fruits, vegetables, meats—eating a variety of foods. Just stay away from your Twinkies—unless it is for dessert—and by that time you'll have what you need. And get lots of exercise! Keep that weight under control because we all have—I think you need a proper diet. I really do. I try to keep us on a fairly decent schedule. And it used to be I'd talk to our prenatal girls and tell them diet is really important and young girls— before they are of childbearing age—it is important that they eat properly. They are then building their bones and this will go on for the next generation. And their teeth. Drink milk. We still believe in milk. **CLC:** And we have seen the improvement, believe me, in children's teeth. Used to be they had little black spots here and all through here. And when you'd examine them before they'd first go to school, you'd see that Now they are all white and pretty. **SH:** See, they didn't have dental care. **CLC:** And they had no fluoride in the water. And they'd get that treatment in school. Things like that made a big difference in children's teeth.

SG: *What about children's diseases? What have you seen change? Why, I remember taking my children for sugar cubes—Salk vaccine. But I can remember summers when my little friends got polio.* **SH:** That was a dreadful time. **CLC:** I hated summer. **SH:** Hated summer because of polio.

SG: *Did you see it here?* **CLC:** We saw this boy, and we knew he had polio. **SH:** You know Steve Young? It was his brother. His brother died of polio. **CLC:** And you walked in that room and you saw him sitting there, and you knew. **SH:** His mother was one, you know, who worried in particular about her children getting polio. They were having everything done right for them. And I can remember that child got sick on a Sunday, and she called about noon, and we went right over when we finished eating, and that child had polio. **CLC:** You could tell him just sitting in the bed. We sent him to Lexington that very day. They put him on a respirator that night, and then he died. **SH:** But that's what happened to children. They'd just be sick a day or two and die.

SG: *Have you seen many children die?* **CLC:** More than my share. **SH:**

Well, I can think of one—oh, those two. Well, they were already dead. Two. It was carbon monoxide poisoning. **CLC**: Oh, yes, Lord. **SH**: They were driving through here in a car, and they had these three children. One was in the front seat and two were asleep in the back. One started vomiting, so they stopped. They were going through here in the middle of the night, and we saw this child and it was vomiting, and you could tell immediately it was from carbon monoxide. Its lips were all red. But, anyway, it got better right away. And Louise asked them, "Where are the other children?" And they said, "Asleep on the floor of the car." And we went out there, and they were dead.

SG: *They pulled up to your office?* **CLC**: No, at Mother's. We were living at Mother's then. **SH**: This was about two o'clock in the morning. Another time we had a girl going through here with her parents and her husband, and she was on her way to West Virginia. She was in labor, active labor. They stopped. So we put her right into Louise's mother's bed, and we kept her overnight. Well, they were from somewhere in Tennessee, and they hadn't been married long enough, and they were very proud people. This was crazy to begin with. She had that baby in Louise's mother's bed. **CLC**: Well, but then we couldn't get 'em to leave. After the baby was born, they wouldn't leave. I think it was two or three days before we ever did get them out! **SH**: They were these southern people who thought you shouldn't move a muscle after you had a baby. You stayed in bed for two weeks or something— right, no matter whose bed. **CLC**: Oh, it was something! **SH**: Now, that was a strange experience to get on from nutrition and health.

SG: *And now the dreaded subject—smoking. [To Louise.] You started when?* **CLC**: I didn't smoke until I went to college, and I actually didn't smoke then. I used to play at the sorority house and got a corncob pipe and smoked that. I didn't really get the bad habit 'til med school. **SH**: And it was fashionable at that time. During the war, cigarettes were big then. **CLC**: And all of the boys, you know, all of us in med school— they'd bring in these big boxes, like that—cartons of cigarettes and everybody got 'em so if you didn't smoke, well. So, I had three or four cartons. Yes, the cigarette companies gave big boxes to medical students. **SH**: See, I think most of the men were in the military in the 1940s, and they always gave cigarettes to the military. **CLC**: There was only one in my whole class that wasn't in the military. There were two girls and three boys. **SH**: I don't think the cigarette companies, in the beginning, knew that it wasn't good for you. **CLC**: That wasn't considered a health problem really—smoking. **SH**: Not at that time. But I think that was the beginning of the health problem.

SG: *How much would you smoke when you really got into it?* **CLC:** All the time I was awake!

SG: *Can I put that in?* **CLC:** That was the truth. Now, when I quit, I woke up at three o'clock in the morning to smoke a cigarette and I said to myself, "Now, Louise, you don't need that." So I didn't smoke it. I went back to bed, and I went to sleep. I woke up the next morning, and I said, "Now, Louise, you went by that cigarette last night," and I didn't smoke one. Then I had breakfast, and I didn't smoke one after that. **SH:** I about fainted. **CLC:** She'd try to get me to stop. It would go around in your mind, you know, but you have to hit something that says, "This is it." But I tell you, I couldn't breathe and I coughed. . . . I quit fourteen years ago. Yes, I like to smoke. **SH:** I didn't smoke, but I'd light them for her in the car, and we were in the ruts and I'd light them for her, but I never did buy them. But it did bother me sitting at a table and it would blow in my direction. **CLC:** Only advice about smoking: If you don't start, you won't have to stop. [Laughs.] And you won't know how much fun it was, either. But you don't need to know that.

SG: *Who gave you that bunny?* **CLC:** The Sisters [at the hospital].

SG: *Has that bunny got a name?* **CLC:** Just bunny. It snuggles. [She hugs the stuffed bunny.]

Jane Caudill
June 17, 1993

Jane Caudill is the widow of Louise's beloved brother Boone (August 22, 1915-August 11, 1970). Jane was born in Indiana on November 17, 1917. She has always been the strong support of the Caudill family, and it is through her son Proctor and his three sons that the Caudill name will continue.

Jane Caudill lives across the street from the big white Caudill family home. Many of Louise and Susie's memories are closely bound up with Jane Caudill and her house, from Susie's first memories of Morehead and being picked up by Jane at the station, to their daily use of Jane's washing machine when they came back from deliveries in the country. Jane has played, and still does play, a unifying role in the Caudill family.

I met Louise on New Year's Eve, 1939. That was at Lucille's in Lexington. I'm from southern Indiana. I met Boone when he was in law school and I was working. We married in 1939. I didn't meet any of the family until that New Year's Eve. Lucille was married to Paul Little then. We went to a cotillion. Then the next day Granny and Pa Caudill came, so I met the whole family. And I was very apprehensive about meeting the family. All of them were very gracious to me. Well, we all had to get dressed to go to that daggone cotillion. We wore formal gowns; at that time we all did. It was an annual thing. We had a good time. But that was my first time to meet Louise. I felt real comfortable. I don't know how she felt.

Louise and Lucille were so different then. They've always been different. Well, Lucille is older and I think she tried to take care of Weezer. I've always called Louise "Weezer," and in a way, I think Lucille may have felt a little bit responsible [for her]. Boone was not like either of his sisters.

And then I met their parents. I call them Granny and Pa. They lived right across the street. See, Boone and I lived in that family home for seven or eight years after we were married in 1939. Granny and Pa were so good to me. My mother died a couple years after Boone and I married, and Granny was just my Mommy. And Pa Caudill, bless his heart, he was a business man. But he liked to play checkers and pool and bridge and read. Granny took care of us. Oh, [Pa] was the provider and so forth, but Granny just kind of held everything together. You would have loved her. A cute little lady. They were awfully nice to me and I tried to return it . . . and so nice to my children, Susie, Etta Jane, Proc, and Sally. Proc and Bobby [Roberta Hough] live here in the outskirts of Morehead. They have three boys, Boone, Aaron, and Ben.

I met Susie Halbleib at Oneida, Kentucky, at the little maternity hospital there. And it was on New Year's Eve in 1947. Boone and I were invited to come over to see them for New Year's Eve. And it was the dickens getting there. Muddy roads and we didn't know the way. We finally got there just before the New Year's Eve was over. They were delivering a baby. Oh, it was fun! They brought the baby in and had tied a red bow around that little teeny tiny infant. And we all had New Year's Eve and told jokes and there were other nurses there.

At first Boone and I were living and working at the People's Bank at Sandy Hook, Kentucky. I still work there, oh, yes, and I love it. Boone and I bought this house in 1947, in Morehead, but we built all of this back part on. We were crowded with four kids running in and out. And Weezer and Granny Caudill, they lived right across the street. And Louise's practice was, well, when I first came here, she was in physical education up at the university. That was in 1939 and she started med school in 1943. Then she came back here. She graduated in 1946 and went to Oneida. That's where she met Susie and came back here and began practicing in January of 1948, upstairs. You probably know all about that.

Susie wasn't scared to come at all. Susie's not scared of anything. She's laid back. Susie came here alone on the train and I met her at the station. Louise, I think, was in New York with a Chinese doctor that had been here. I can remember what we had for dinner that night. Roast beef, potatoes, and carrots and slaw. That was before we built this part back here and that's where we ate, in the kitchen. And the four kids were here. But Susie was just as, well, seemed so comfortable.

Anyway, she said she came into our living room and thought she saw blood on our fireplace. Oh, yes, it was catsup. We'd been sleigh-riding the night before, and we'd had hamburgers in the living room and the heat was off, and I remember that.

We lived here when Pa Caudill died in 1967. Boone died in 1970. Heart. I was in the hospital with Boone in Lexington, and we thought he might be doing a little bit better. I was with him in intensive care, and I couldn't call Weezer and the doctor did. That was it. We came home then. And Granny died in 1976.

Granny was not a good driver. You know where this four-way stop is down here at Second Street and Wilson? She never stopped. She went right through it. She got many tickets for double parking. She had to go collect her rent. Have you heard this one? Well, she went to collect the rent—they owned several pieces of property—and she parked in front of the police station one day. They had property right next to the police station. So she went in to collect her rent, and when she came back she had a ticket. So she took it into the police station and said, "I'm not going to pay this. I've just been here a minute or two." So they kind of argued with her and she said, "Just give me another ticket." And they did. Louise and I paid her parking tickets.

The Caudill household was pretty active. They played bridge. Weekends we always played bridge. Sometimes we played all night, and whoever lost had to wash the dishes. Very competitive people. And there was their sister Patty and brother Bud. He's in Monticello. There's Cille, Weezer, Boone, Buddy, and Pat. Buddy was a terrific athlete, very likable, and a good ole boy.

But Weezer and I have been awfully close and particularly since Boone died. Weezer has helped me a lot. There were times when I needed someone, and I could always go to Weezer. We've never had—oh, we don't agree on everything—and Weezer, well, her influence on people is the fact that she can make people listen to her. To me, that's the thing in her practice that she has done. And Susie, bless her heart, they have gobs of people down there, and Weezer will sit down and talk to someone and make them feel better, and there may be fifteen people out there wanting the same thing. That's Weezer's big thing—listening and talking to people. Also, her love for this hospital and the people she serves. It's real.

Well, Louise and I are awfully close. Yes, I feel she is really my sister, too, and I hope she would say the same thing about me and put it that way. And Susie, too—well, Weezer and I have talked about this—because Susie is a strong person. She's had a lot of tragedy in her family. Susie was raised by her grandmother. She is one of five, and she is the eldest. She just has sort of helped her family. Weezer couldn't make it without Susie. No way.

Weezer is not a fancy person, and she likes tailored slacks and, of course, she can't play tennis anymore, but I bought her tennis shorts. Now, they both love the house and they both like to be comfortable, but I don't think they need a daggone thing as an addition. I tried to buy them a microwave. Why, they didn't want one! I don't know where they'd put it. Probably in the bathroom. They are not interested in modern appliances. Well, they have everything they need. Louise is very appreciative of what she has, and if she wants something, she gets it. And Susie is the same thing. Now, Susie likes dresses. Oh, and Weezer loves jewelry. Oh, she likes jewels. She really does. And she likes to dress up.

Yes, I think a lot of people would be disturbed or scared or insecure if she closed up her practice, and I think she worries about that. I think that's why she is staying on—up to a point. I think now she has begun to think about herself some. Oh, sure, she is my doctor, too. I know of doctors in Lexington who have said that Louise is one of the best diagnosticians that they have known. I mean, she might be diagnosing something, but if she were not sure, she would send them on. Usually they concurred with her.

And Weezer's thing has been about people and about getting the hospital. She's a people person. She's different. You don't forget her. What is it about her? I don't know the word. But there's only one of her. I guess it's her caring. She has some sort of charisma that draws you to her and you feel comfortable.

Now, on the other hand, Louise is very timid. Boone was timid. Boone and Louise were very much alike. She doesn't like to be in crowds, and Boone didn't either. Boone and Weezer were the nearest alike of the five kids. She really is timid, and Boone was, and my son, Proc, he is, too. And they all do have personality qualities, but down deep they are timid. They kind of sit back—don't want to take the spotlight. No, not out of fear. Louise is the one to reach out to someone who might be timid and tries to make them comfortable. She does that, but it depends on the situation. Okay, if there were twelve people in this room right now, Louise would not be the leader. What I mean is, she would not be the one who comes in and says, "How's everybody and what are we doing tonight?" Boone was that way, and Proc is that way. Now, I'm not. I'll just get things going. And I'm, well, it's personality differences. But when things get started, they all get into it. You can see that in Weezer. You know she is outgoing and so forth, but she's not one to hold the floor. Susie is a very humble person. And genuine. Proc and I talk about it a lot—how gracious she is. Susie is just a fine, fine person.

And, oh, yes, they delivered Sally right here in this house on Thanksgiving Day. We had a ball. Right here in that bedroom. We planned it. Sally was the youngest of our four. All the others were born in a hospital, and that was before the hospital here. So Louise and Susie asked me, and I said, "That's fine with me." Now, they were teetotally scared to death. Both of them. I wasn't, oh, no.

I called them up about three o'clock in the morning. See, my water broke the week before and I was working. Anyway, on Wednesday—why, I'm telling you the life story of all of us—on Wednesday, Weezer said, "Well, we'll probably have it tonight." So I called them and they came over. They lived in the family home across the street at that time, and they got right in bed with me. Yes, Weezer and Susie both got in bed with me! They were so tired. Now, the children were singing at the church in the choir, Susie and Etta Jane. The two oldest were singing in the church, so I combed their hair and tied their bows and they went off to church and came back and they had a baby sister. Boone was here taking care of Proc. He was a nervous wreck, yes. I thought he'd like to die.

Oh, and Louise and Susie used to go out on deliveries all night long. Then they'd come back to the people all lined up on the stairs here. But they came first to our house to do the laundry. Well, it was called packs, delivery packs, and we never locked our doors then, and they'd come in— say 1, 2, 3, or 4 a.m. and put something in my wash machine. Granny didn't have a wash machine. I'd get them out the next morning and put them in the dryer. Sometimes they'd have three or four. And these were big packs and all that stuff you drape with.

So Sally was born, I think, about nine in the morning. Now this was three in the morning when I called them, and they came over and got in bed with me. Proc was crying. Anyway, I was just as calm as a cucumber. But they were as nervous as a whore in church. They just put their little portable table on the bed. They did all the prenatal care. Yes, they were scared because it was me. Well, put yourself in their place. So I took a shower about an hour and a half later and we had Thanksgiving dinner. It was a fun time, and when the kids came home from church on Thanksgiving morning, they had a little sister and they went running up and down this street yelling they had a little sister. About two o'clock I had a can of beer!

Well, I don't see Weezer as much as I used to because of driving back and forth to Sandy Hook, where I work at People's Bank, but I talk to her every night. I call her at five minutes after seven every night. And we go to the same church.

A healer? Well, I don't think that in her own concept of herself she feels that way. She loves to please. I'll tell you another thing about Weezer, and I think this is characteristic of many. You have to keep your self-esteem going. I think she doesn't really realize how much she has helped people. I guess I would say she is humble and she does what she does because that's what she does. She doesn't *have* to do it.

Dr. James Quisenberry
June 26, 1993

Dr. James Quisenberry (born January 31, 1932) was the first to suggest Dr. Louise to me as a physician and the first to tell me of her virtues, but said she did not take new patients. He also remarked, as did so many others, that Dr. Louise still keeps current on everything in the medical field. He said her house was piled with medical journals. As her next-door neighbor, he would know, I assumed.

Today, Dr. Quisenberry is a retired professor of speech from Morehead State University and still lives in Morehead in his house on a high hill that overlooks Dr. Louise's tennis court--where she taught his children to play.

When we came here in the fall of 1968, we were expecting our first child and no other doctor was taking OB/GYN cases, and so Louise became our family doctor by default. We moved here in August, and Lynn was born in November, and in her six-week check-up Dr. Louise caught a heart condition, a murmur that is not ordinarily caught until a six-month check-up. Louise referred us to Dr. Jacqueline Noonen, a pediatric cardiologist at the University of Kentucky, and the X rays proved Louise's diagnosis, that Lynn had a hole between the two bottom chambers of her heart. Now, Jacqueline Noonen is one of the outstanding pediatric cardiologists in the nation, and so we felt like Lynn was in the best hands possible. Now, Louise and Susie had planned a vacation in Hawaii; instead of going to Hawaii, Louise took that time to go to Johns Hopkins for a special seminar on Lynn's condition. And so that kind of dedication is very moving. Nobody can say a bad thing to me about Louise Caudill. That's the kind of a lady she is. I just found out about what she did accidentally. Maybe Susie mentioned something about that. It was just most reassuring to find somebody who practiced medicine that way.

Obstetrics was her big thing. She was great with it. I asked her one time, I said, "Why is it that you don't just specialize in OB/GYN and baby deliveries?" She said, "I like to know my baby's family history. I like to treat the whole family. Then you know what to look for." And I guess that is what has made her one of the finest diagnosticians around. I went in there one day and my chest was just killing me and I knew that I had pleurisy. Well, she listened and then she said, "You haven't got pleurisy." So I said,

"Well, what on earth is the matter with me?" She said, "About three days ago you had the dry heaves and you made your muscles sore." And she was right. That's what had happened. She's just a marvelous diagnostician.

Once I had this little twist in my back and went to her for that to check it out and she said, "Now, somebody may tell you scoliosis, but I don't think so. I think you've got a fatty tumor on your left shoulder blade. But I am going to send you to a specialist." So I went to the specialist and came back and he's diagnosed a fatty tumor. And I told her that I'd found out the difference between a specialist and a general practitioner. And she asked, "What's that?" And I said, "About thirty-five dollars on that office call."

But that's the way she practices medicine, and she has diagnosed every condition that I ever had and then sent me on to a specialist who'd just confirm her diagnosis. But she has never missed on me or on any member of my family. She delivered Lynn in 1968, so from August of 1968 she has been our family doctor and will continue to be until she hangs up her practice.

And the amazing thing to me is that she lives where she lives because of a case. The fellow who owned this land had two children; both of whom had multiple sclerosis. Louise built her house next door to them and so close to them that they shared a driveway, so she could get to those children any hour of the day or night, so she could do everything that could be done. The little boy lived to be about twelve. He loved horses and he wanted to ride in the world's grand champion horse show at the Kentucky State Fair. And Louise fixed him up with medications enough that he was able to ride at what he called his "World's Fair." He always wanted to ride in the World's Fair and he did, and I think he died less that six weeks after that. But she managed to get him there.

She lived there so she could care for them. She is the most compassionate person I've ever known. She says that she is just doing her job and that's her phrase. Yes, she says she just does what she has to do, but that's because of who she is. Nobody holds anything over her head. It is her own motivation.

Now, there was a time when she was a power here in her political affiliations. I don't know if she is still active or not, but I know she was one of the first members on the Council on Higher Education. She was a member of that and active in that. She does many things and is active in many ways that never get out because she thinks that is part of her job, too, just like building a hospital here was a job that needed to be done and Louise could do it.

When I came here in 1968, phase I of that hospital was there. Now we've got phase III. Phase II was opened when Lynn was about four or five years old, and we were there for that grand opening. Well, Dr. Warren Proudfoot came walking by. Now, Dr. Louise was Lynn's GP, Jacqueline Noonen was her pediatric cardiologist, and Marie Brossey was her dentist. So when Warren Proudfoot walked by and I spoke to him, Lynn asked who that was. And I told her it was Dr. Proudfoot. She said, "Oh, he can't be a real doctor. He's a man!"

We've just had a marvelous relationship. Susie is almost as good at medicine as Louise is. Louise told me one time, she said, "Susie knows everything I know about being a doctor, but I don't know everything she knows about being a nurse." Susie's just great!

But they are not just our neighbors. They are dear friends, and we just count on them. Her house was here when I came here. We built this house. We bought the land from the same fellow that she bought her property from [Elijah Hogge]. I didn't know her house was there when I bought this land. I'll tell you what, Lige had decided not to sell this land off. By then he decided he'd sell off these front lots here. The Sunday before Lynn was born we drove by here, saw this For Sale sign on that lot, and I thought, well, that's a beautiful place. Lynn was born on a Monday and on Tuesday, while she was still in the hospital, I asked to buy it. He said, well, he had so many friends who wanted first refusal on it--so maybe the best thing to do would be to sell it to a stranger, and then "all my friends won't be mad at me." But he said, "I'm going to do one more thing." He asked me if I knew Louise Caudill, and I said yes, I did. He said, "She's my neighbor and will be your next-door neighbor, and I'm going to ask her if it's all right with her for me to sell to you." So he got on the phone and called and told me, "She'd as soon have you as anybody." That was the first time I knew that they were going to be our next-door neighbors. She didn't ask if we played tennis, but she taught Lynn how to play tennis on her courts. She taught a lot of kids to play tennis. They were so busy, but we'd run in over there every once in a while. On a Sunday afternoon she would have her medical journals spread out all over. When she drives to work she's got a cassette player in her automobile, and she is constantly playing tapes to keep her updated on her profession. She stays current.

One of the pharmacists told me not long ago that Louise is still prescribing medicines before they are supplied to the pharmacists. She will find out that they are coming out and she'll prescribe them and the pharmacist will have to special order them. And she is very conscientious about her pharmacology, and she won't give you one medication without checking every medication you are taking. She said, "I will never give you more than two without checking everything. You know what one may do to another one, but when you put a third one there, you never know."

I still go to her. Oh, yes, I was there two weeks ago. My ears were all stopped up and I thought I was going stone deaf. Well, she took one look and got them all cleaned up, and now the television set can play back where it used to. I had it so loud the neighbors could hear it. I don't really know what I would do for a physician without her. I'm sure there are other good physicians here. She is always my first stop.

As for her family and her presence, I don't know what this town would have been. She is a public servant because that was her daddy, too. He was one of the main figureheads and an unsung hero in bringing Morehead State University to this town. He worked on the committee with Fields and with Allie Young, and he was more or less the one who didn't make the front-page headlines. But he worked with them as diligently as they did. And that's why we have Morehead State University. And that is Morehead's major employer, and the second major employer is St. Claire Medical Center. So Morehead would be like some of our neighboring counties with double-digit unemployment instead of being where it is. That is just for an economic standpoint. I think I would be safe in saying that half the teachers in eastern Kentucky come from Morehead State University. Then when you consider that this hospital here is considered competitive with anything you have today in Lexington, I think that that was her pushing for quality. No doubt about that. She just absolutely demanded of her hospital what she demanded of herself. And that is doing her job to the best of her ability. And even today, you can see this.

From my church now, I am in and out of the hospital to visit all of the time. That staff still reflects Louise and Susie's personalities. They like each other, and there is always a smile, and they are cordial and congenial. Because of Louise, that attitude grows. You know, as the twig is bent, so grows the tree. The same thing goes for an institution when it is founded on certain principles. They beget their own and employ people like themselves, with the same sort of philosophy, and she is very much responsible for that.

I think that bus crash is what united everyone. When people saw the kind of care that was given, that this hospital showed, people realized that this was a matter of compassion that the Sisters showed, and the volunteer pastors and assistants at the hospital are Protestants. We sign up, and when someone of our faith is in the hospital, they call us.

I think Louise's dedication came from her dad, and I don't know where he got his. You know, I think a lot is how we first perceive opportunities and how we look at them as opportunities or challenges. I think a lot of it comes from ourselves. We do all we think that we can do. As Henry Ford said, "When a man thinks he can or can't, he's right." If he thinks he can, he does, and if he thinks he can't, he gives up on the first try. I really believe that the most essential thing for success is the belief in ourselves. And Louise has, too, a belief in a God who will empower us to be all that we can be. I don't think Louise worries about whether or not she is successful. Success is achieving; it is not arriving at a certain point in time. I think Louise's idea of success is in terms of personal satisfaction, the top of the Maslow scale [for her].

When she talks to you, you are her center of attention as a total human being. She's a sociologist, a humanitarian, and a friend all in one. She is not just diagnosing a patient or a condition. She is treating the whole person because she cares about you.

Dr. Claire Louise Caudill, Susie Halbleib, and Dr. Travis Preston Lockhart

May 20, 1993

By the time of this interview, arrangements were being made by Morehead State University to produce the play I was planning. Dr. Louise and Susie were well aware of this plan and probably felt some shyness about their lives being portrayed on stage. They graciously agreed, however. Dr. Lockhart, director of MSU Theatre, was welcomed for this interview, too, as he was to direct me in the play and did not really know Dr. Louise and Susie.

We knew we had to begin thinking about staging the play and were more than a little anxious. But we also knew we were in a situation that must be rare in theater. Here were the subjects of a play, the playwright, and the director in the same room and able to discuss ideas and plans.

CLC: Oh, listen, I had a real experience this week! A man came in and showed me his finger and he said, "Did you know you sewed this finger on twenty-six years ago?" He said, "You know, I came up and I had cut it off. And you said, 'Where's the other piece?' and I said, 'Well, my wife knows where it is.' So she went back and brought the finger in." Daggone, it took, and he has a fingernail now and everything! **SH:** It looks great. **CLC:** It just looks like a finger. Oh, and we have put an ear on, I can remember that. I think we had two ears. Suz, there was one, I think, that a horse bit an ear off and swallowed that ear. And you know what Mother said? She said, "They ought to kill that horse." But the other one was in a fight and . . . **SH:** Oh, yes, a human did it! **CLC:** Yes, a human did it! So there were two ear stories.

SG: *Did he just come in holding his ear?* **SH:** Yes. **CLC:** You'd be surprised how well they grow quite often. **SH:** Even with feelings. It is surprising.

SG: *The first time I came here, I met some people named Hogge who used to live right next door to you. They had two children with a disease.* **CLC:** Cystic fibrosis. That affects the pancreas and the lungs. They usually die of pneumonia or something like that.

SG: *Well, somebody told me that you built this house right here so that* *you could be near those children.* **CLC:** Yes, he was a Hogge [Elijah Hogge], and he was a lawyer. They had ties with Cleveland and Texas; they took the children every place.

SG: *For health, for medicine?* **CLC:** For medicine, yes. They went wherever there was a center that knew anything about cystic fibrosis.

SG: *Why would you have to have closeness? Emergencies?* **CLC:** We didn't have to. But he [the son, Rowe] would get to the place where he was like an asthmatic, you know. He couldn't breathe. I'll never forget the last time we saw him. He wanted to ride in what he called the World's Fair. That was a big fair [in Louisville], and he loved to ride his horse.

SG: *The little boy, how old was he?* **CLC:** He was about ten, no, twelve. He started out and got as far as Owingsville and he couldn't breathe, so they brought him back. And we just loaded him up on cortisone and he got to ride. We knew we had to give him whatever we could so he could ride in that World's Fair. It was awful important to him, so whatever it took, we did it.

SG: *I'd like to ask you more about one statement in the first interview. You said, "I believe that affect is more important than intelligence." Could you talk about that?* **CLC:** Affect? Well, affect is that thing that makes you feel about something. It isn't what you know about it. It's the feeling of it, and it is the interpretation that you believe yourself. It's not— oh, this is the way it was back in so and so and we did this and that—that's knowledge, facts. And facts, you need a few of them, but if you can't get the feel of them, it wouldn't be any good. Affect is your utility of what you have within.

TL: *It's a human thing? You can't just go to medical school and come out and then that's all there is to it. I mean, if I go to a doctor, I want more than just his or her knowledge of what I have. I want to be cared for. That's it, isn't it?* **CLC:** Yes, cared for. And we don't have enough knowledge. In medicine, we're way off of all knowledge. But I don't mean to damn knowledge, and I think knowledge is important. I wish I had a lot more of it.

SG: *When we started out, there were a lot of things I wasn't ready to think about yet and now we have to—like a stage set, like music, or clothes— all those things you have to do to put a play together. Is there a kind of music that you like?* **CLC:** I tell you, I thought the *Rhapsody in Blue* the other night was wonderful. And I went to Lexington to hear the music from *Oklahoma* and really enjoyed that very much.

SG: *Broadway musicals. What about when you come home tired at the end of a day, do you put on music?* **CLC:** We usually go swimming. I used to play tennis all the time. I'd play five hours on Wednesdays.

SG: *Do you play tennis, too, Susie?* **SH:** I do, but not five hours!

SG: *Do you play anymore?* **CLC:** I have a little trouble. My legs don't work anymore. As I look at it, surely to the Lord, I was better back then than I am now.

SG: *I remember you telling me that years ago you had to walk up those hills and that was hard.* **SH:** She was a smoker.

SG: *She says it was her legs. You say it was her smoking.* **SH:** But they go together. **CLC:** You don't get any air. Well, it got worse as time went on. **SH:** But you've done pretty good for all the years you did smoke. **CLC:** Yes, and I smoked hard.

SG: *What do you mean by* hard? **CLC:** Well, you know those people who take a little bitty smoke and then let the cigarette rest in the ashtray? Not me! I'd take a great big drag, like that, get it down in my lungs good, and then I'd blow it out. Y'all, it was wonderful.

SG: *Did you smoke tough cigarettes, too, like Camels and Phillip Morris?* **CLC:** Oh, Pall Malls, and for a long time I smoked those things like brown paper—to cure smoking. Wet brown paper. That's what Carltons taste like. I smoked them for two or three years. They are the worst tasting thing you could ever imagine.

SG: *They're supposed to be the lowest in nicotine.* **CLC:** That's why I smoked 'em. They were terrible.

TL: *How did you quit? Did you just stop?* **CLC:** I got up one morning, three o'clock, and came in here to smoke a cigarette and I just gave myself a talk and said, "Louise, you don't need that cigarette." So I went back to bed and as soon as I got out of bed I started and thought about last night and didn't have that one, and so the last cigarette I didn't have was the last one I didn't have.

SG: *But were you feeling the effects of it by that time? When you said, "I don't need it," you must have felt something.* **CLC:** I'd have coughing spasms so bad they would disturb the whole church. That wasn't good for a doctor.

SG: *Oh, my, if you chainsmoked, how were you delivering babies? What did you do in your office?* **CLC:** I smoked in the office. You know, I don't see how people could stand me 'cause I smelled like a drain—was bound to. Because now, when somebody smokes, it really gets me.

SG: *I don't know how we got on this from music! [Laughs]* **CLC:** How about "Smoke Gets in Your Eyes"?

SG: *Every time we start here we end up over there. Okay, music, back to music. Let's say they want to use music to open the show, or during intermission. What music would you identify?* **SH:** I think we'd have to be thinking about it.

SG: *By the same token, are there any hymns that you are particularly fond of?* CLC: Oh, I do that almost every Sunday morning. I go through the hymn book and decide which ones I'll have for my funeral. I guess you'd have to give us homework to do that. I'll make you a list.

SG: *I'm also trying to think of what would be the big conflict in your life. I remember those letters when you were having a hard time getting the hospital the way you wanted it to be. It seems to me that would have been something you really fought for and believed in.* SH: But in reality it didn't come to that. CLC: Well, we had to leave a lot of it out, but we got the structure. . . . I wanted the hospital to have in it all the specialists. I wanted the general practitioners to send the people to the hospital for the specialists: cardiologists, neurologists, and so forth. And when they got through with them, got them well, they send them back to the family practitioner. That was the kind of setup that we had in mind. And there's lots of reasons why it wouldn't work—because the specialists would all be paid the same salary. We found out some places that had had that. There were some problems with our idea, too. The specialists wouldn't always do what you wanted 'em to. And too, the practitioner might not be able to pick up what was wrong in order to get them to the specialist. I mean, there were problems with it. Even though I think it's a good idea, well, you have to get an awful lot of people to agree with you. You have to have a lot of people who have that "affect."

SG: *So it was hard to find, at that time here in Morehead, people who were supportive of what you wanted to do.* CLC: Well, see, our plan was made by Dr. Willard and Bob Johnson and Dr. Pellegrino, Dr. Segnitz and myself. We're the ones who figured out what we thought it ought to be. They were all from New Jersey. Came to University of Kentucky. See, they were starting the med school there the same time we were building this hospital. So they were interested in the med school as being a part of this community hospital. So they were willing to just give, oh, almost anything. Willard and Bob Johnson came to all our meetings for, I'd say, two or three years and, honey, that's a lot for a dean of a med school. But there was a hospital—Hunterdon—that they knew had sort of some of these ideas. They had this idea of the family practitioner and specialists on the hospital staff. Susie and I went up there with Dr. Segnitz and Sister Mary Edwin, who was about my age—just the four of us. And we went to their meetings and to see how they did things. We could sort of see that some of our ideas weren't working too good there.

SG: *So you saw the ideas you had actually in practice and they weren't working?* **CLC:** Well, they weren't fully working. You knew you had to do something to improve on it, though.

SG: *Did you get your concept from them, or did it just happen that they matched?* **CLC:** A little bit of both. I think Dean Willard had understood the way they ran it up there, and he wanted something sort of like that. And Dr. Segnitz, he called every night about 3 a.m. We'd talk for an hour or two. **SH:** That's true. He was great on the telephone, but he was busy all day long.

SG: *So when you proposed these ideas you couldn't get the doctors to come here. They wouldn't agree to get paid all the same salary?* **CLC:** Well, they did. The ones that came in the very beginning. But it didn't take us long to see that a surgeon has to have more money than an internist. **SH:** They just bring in more money.

TL: *It's just economics, isn't it?* **CLC:** In education it's that way. Certain fields are sort of looked up to, whether they make more money or not. I know that when I was a P.E. teacher, you were the lowest one on the totem pole. That's just the way that life deals out the cards.

SG: *Of course, in any field there are people who work hard and those who just loaf by, which wrecks plans.* **CLC:** That's why, when you've got the human element, you've got to look pretty deep.

SG: *There's probably a lot of law we wouldn't need, either. So your ideal hospital never happened.*

TL: *You were asking for a certain amount of sacrifice. Sometimes that goes beyond human nature.* **CLC:** You'd be surprised. There's a man who is going to come next year in surgery. He wants to come and his wife does, too. It's really a big deal that both of them want to come and work and you don't make as much money here as you do in Lexington or Louisville. But my philosophy was that there's a lot of people that just want to live calm and easy. Make a living, being well satisfied with what you make doing what you want to do. Not make five million a year. One person said that to me: "Just make a living." It's funny that women will do that, but most of the women aren't married and don't have a family responsibility. So I think that doesn't give women the total edge.

SG: *What about idealism? The kid that says, "I want to be a doctor and help mankind." Does that really exist?* **CLC:** Yes, I think it does. **SH:** I think the dean of the school of medicine right now is doing his best to instill that to the students. **CLC:** He's good. Why, he said some mighty good words about me. **SH:** Med school graduation. She almost didn't go to that. She'd gotten a doctorate down at UK last year. Then Dr. Wilson invited her to come to the med school graduation. Well, she thought, I guess it's customary when you get an honorary degree to do that, so she agreed to do it. Then when the time really came she thought, well, I really—oh, it doesn't make any difference, maybe I won't go. It was on a Sunday. It's just a good thing she did go. No, I didn't know, either. Jane and I were just absolutely beside ourselves. He said so many nice things.

SG: *We were talking about stage sets. I think they want something elaborate—and I'm trying to think of a set for you. Tennis court, swimming pool. I thought of that one room in your office that is all full of baby pictures. You know, where you sit on a stool and write your unreadable prescriptions. Again, how many babies do you think you delivered?*
CLC: Susie figured eight thousand. I swear I can't count that many.
SH: Well, I didn't really count that many, but I gave them the ones we'd delivered in the office. But I couldn't give them all the ones we delivered out in the area because all those birth certificates were gone. And then I figured what we delivered at the hospital. Oh, somebody else figured that out, I guess. No, I just figured what I could.

SG: *If there were a second set—well, Travis and I have been talking a lot, so we went up to your cemetery that you took me to. It was the most beautiful day.* CLC: It is a beautiful view.

TL: *The first year I was here I discovered it, and that really is one of the most beautiful scenes I've ever seen. It's not just the mountains and so forth. It's also down into the town. I've been up there every now and then when I needed some kind of uplift. But I didn't know the significance.* CLC: My grandfather lived over in Clearfield, and he could see that hill from where he lived. That's where he decided that he wanted it.

TL: *It seems so untouched. It doesn't look like anybody goes up there and messes it up.*

SG: *I was thinking that that would make a beautiful stage set in the sense that you are up on that hill and in the back are the mountains and down below is Morehead. Travis thought maybe that could be a "downer" to some people—open in a cemetery. But you don't feel like that up there.*

TL: *Oh, I don't think that is necessarily true.* SH: I don't think so, either.
CLC: Susie drives everybody up there. SH: Oh, I do. It's wonderful.

SG: *What would you think of that? As a matter of fact, if you remember when I first started to write this I had it set in the cemetery and I had never even seen that cemetery at that time. It seemed to me a wonderful way to talk about your family and then talk about the town because it is right in that setting, too.*

TL: *Now, there are ways to incorporate more than one image on the stage. We don't have to limit it to one set—with the office and the cemetery.*

We can do a lot of different things. But I could envision, for example, the play beginning, and I could envision the ending—then to the office—then to wherever. And the combination of not only the set but lighting could take you anywhere you want to go. So we really don't have to be talking about one place only or another place only. There are ways to get several of them. But the more I thought about it, the more I thought about that setting up there as a kind of, oh, like bookends. You know, this as sort of a framework, this is where we start and then end and it could be quite beautiful. . . . Of course, depending on how it's written, but that's a beautiful image. It really is.

SG: *It's what I first had in my head as a way for you to talk about your family, about the whole town, and then to close there, too. But I had no idea about that cemetery when I wrote that and so when I saw it, it seemed a bit like fate. Maybe this is just how it has to be.* **CLC:** It's plain.

TL: *But you see, that's what I think of Morehead. In eleven years I've grown to love this place.* **CLC:** Well, good. I don't think there is any place like it.

TL: *You see the mountains and you see the town and you see all that, but it's just there. God did that. It's not pretentious. It's just life. I'd like to see some of that get into this play.*

Jeanne Frances, Sister of Notre Dame,
June 11, 1993

Sister Jeanne Frances (born August 10, 1934, in Covington, Kentucky) of the Order of Notre Dame is probably as good and organized a storyteller as she is a nurse. She gave her interview one morning in the peaceful, immaculate front room of the brick convent house behind the hospital where the Sisters live. I'd had no idea about talking to people at the hospital because I didn't think any of the original Sisters could still be there. I met Jeanne Frances quite by accident—my accident—as I was in the emergency ward after falling and breaking a foot. While we talked, it came out that she was among the original Sisters sent to Morehead to set up the hospital before it even opened. She readily agreed to talk about the early days. This rare and remarkable woman probably is another saint, and she continues to be the guiding light of the emergency ward—night shift. Her story, too, is one of inspiration for any reader.

I belong to the Sisters of Notre Dame. We cannot turn down any poor patients. We were originally founded in France in the middle of the eighteenth century. See, these two rich girls in Germany refused to go to school because their poor friends couldn't go with them. So they got a home and started a school taking in the poor children, educating them, teaching them everything imaginable—a lot of domestic work in the house, sewing and cooking and that—and teaching them how to read and write. Then a priest came along and said, "Hey, you are living the religious life. Why don't you think about taking the vows?"

They decided to go ahead, and they got three of the French Notre Dames to come over and live with them and tell them more about religious life. By then, three more joined them, and after several years, the French Notre Dames went back because they started this school in Germany. We're considered to be for the poor Germans, but in the time of Hitler there was a community over here in the United States, and Hitler was exiling all the Sisters from Germany. And they said, "Why don't you come over here? There's plenty for you to do in America." The Sisters arrived on July 4. They heard all the firecrackers and thought at first that that was for their coming! Then they stayed in New York for a little while.

Then they heard a priest from Covington say, "Hey, there's a lot of work to be done out here in Covington, Kentucky. Come on down." That's how we got started down here in Kentucky. Then about 1950, there was a hospital in Lynch, Kentucky, that nobody was running. It's down on the Tennessee border, I think. So our Sisters—we had several nurses—they went down there and took over the Lynch hospital. But then Danville built a great big new community hospital and the mines were closing in Lynch. It was 1960 and they said, "Well, that will be fine. We can go back to Covington."

At that time, Dr. Louise Caudill decided to go around—she was sending letters to just everybody—to start a hospital here in Morehead. And the equipment in the Lynch hospital, we were just going to move it up or give it away or do anything with it. But we had a lot of equipment, and we were packing up at the time. But Dr. Louise sent a letter to Bishop Towell. He was in charge of the Catholic Hospital Association of Northern Kentucky and the area. He got a letter from this little Morehead, Kentucky, and he thought, "No way could conditions be like she says they are."

He thought they must have been very poor and she needed a lot of help. She was working day and night and just needed somebody else. She wanted to start a hospital so that the poor people didn't have to go so far, being so sick. She either had to send them to Lexington or to Ashland, and she said that many of the people were so sick that they almost died on the way—or did die on the way, because they didn't make it. There were bad roads and everything. So he thought, oh, conditions can't be like that. So he came to Morehead, unannounced, with his secretary and just walked into Louise's office. And that morning, the way I understood, and he said he'll never know where she got five babies, but there she had just delivered five babies. And he said when he saw those babies reaching up to him, no way could he say no!

He knew our hospital was closing, so then he came back to Sister Mary Borromeo, who was our Provincial Superior, and he said, "Look, I've got a good deal for you." He said, "You've got nurses, you've got equipment," he said, "and in Morehead they want to build a hospital." So they decided to come down and see, too, and when Sister Borromeo met Dr. Louise, she just fell in love with her, too, and just thought that we would enjoy working in the area. So that's really how we got to Morehead.

And then with our community and with the community here doing fund-raising and that—and they got the Hill-Burton money—and we were able to start the hospital. And then Sister Mary Edwin, who was administrator in Lynch, came down here and Sister Mary Thomasina. Those were the first two who really did the administrative work. Now, I came down with them and opened the hospital. But I was just a practical nurse at the time, and I did more or less all the cleaning and unpacking and the setting up. Then Thomasina started an aides' class, and the aides came and helped us make the beds, put up the window curtains and the bed curtains, and all that. So then it was a real joy.

They said the hospital was finished April 2, 1963. Yes, the building was up, but it was far from being finished. At first we lived in the upstairs, but we had no food and no way to cook food. We lived in the upper corner of the hospital, and we just had sandwiches. And Dr. Louise found out that the kitchen was far from being ready. We had a little electric hot plate for coffee and soup. There were four of us. And she arranged, somehow, in the community that every night they brought us a good hot meal. So for two or three weeks we would go down to the door at six o'clock and there was a good hot meal. Yes, because Dr. Louise noticed.

On the first morning we ate breakfast down in her little two-by-four kitchen in her Main Street office in the back. See, they slept there, they delivered babies there, and everything. At that time she quit delivery out in the country. She built the office and started delivering down there. So the first morning she invited us down there. We had a really good time. Then, during the week, progressively, trucks started coming and delivering things, but they were all union people and we didn't know anybody in the town to help. So I was the youngest and then Thomasina—I was twenty-eight at that time—and Thomasina was there and I would get up in the truck and hand all of the things off while the men sat on the wall. Well, Dr. Louise heard that and she got two men to come and start helping us. And they started helping us clean and we got all that done—like all the initial scrubbing and the washing of the windows.

Now, the contractors' job was to clean, too, but it wasn't as spic and span as we wanted. And that was my first encounter with Dr. Louise. She was here, it seemed, like day and night delivering babies. She'd be here in the mornings just as spry as you please. Susie was right there, too. Anytime. When you call Dr. Louise, you don't ask for Dr. Louise. Susie answers the phone, and Susie was the one—she sort of protected Dr. Louise. But I'd take Susie's orders just the same as I would Louise's. You know if you are hearing from Susie, you are hearing from Dr. Louise. That's how closely associated they were.

I was an LPN [licensed practical nurse] back then. Now I'm an RN, And my first ten years I worked in surgery and the emergency room. I was working here and went back to the University of Kentucky and got my degree from there. We'd stay over there from Monday until Friday morning, and then Friday morning we came back here and worked the weekend. It was Sister Roseanna that was with me.

Here, in Morehead, it was really amazing because most of the people had never encountered religious nuns and, as I say, Sister Claire and I were the two who always went out into the town. And we still wore the full habit then. Oh, yes, that's when we wore the frills all around the face. Oh, yes, black and white ruffles. You can see our pictures in the outreach building. And people, we heard—in fact, we even had to go to the laundromat, and down at the laundromat the man actually took our money and turned it on both sides. They thought that they weren't going to be able to trust us. And we went to the stores and we heard, "Be careful. They are like gypsies. They have big skirts. They can pick up anything." We didn't hear until later—we heard somebody would follow us through the store.

Oh, we weren't used to it, but we just took it as a joke and we knew we had to win over their confidence and prove to them that we were here to help them and to start up a hospital. It didn't take long at all. The Ravenscraft kids and Skipper Holley and the kids from Allen Drive, they came over. They would come under our windows. They'd see the light at night and they'd call out, "Can you come and play?" And we'd go out and toss a ball with them.

Then, well, Skipper Holley was our first bad burn case. At the end of Allen Drive there was a sandpile with a gasoline light on top. He was sitting there, and a kid happened to knock that light over, and then the sand with the gasoline, on him. He was burned pretty bad. We got to know that family very well. They were here quite a while. And Skipper gave me a football for Christmas!

And then, well, they knew they weren't supposed to play in the creek, so Barbara Allen . . . well, they paged me here one day and I came down and Skipper wanted a needle and thread and a Band-Aid. I said, "Skipper, now what do you want this for?" Here they were in that creek bed and Barbara Allen had cut her foot. They wanted to sew it up—fix it before they took her home. Four- and five-year-old kids! So we had to call Mrs. Allen to come over so a doctor could sew up this foot.

So we had a good time. I think that's more or less how it was. We won over the children. Won the families over. The people in the town weren't rude or cruel. They were just real skeptical of us, I think. What are they up to? What are they going to do? And oh, we had so many Catholics signing into the hospital. We had heard that there were only a few Catholics here in Morehead. And here we had many. We heard that people thought they had to be Catholic to get into the hospital! So they were all saying they were Catholic. Yes, like they say it on the form: religious preference. Some have no preference, some say Protestant, some say Church of God. That is on any form anywhere in any hospital. It's so you can get their ministers if you need to. Yes, they thought we would only take care of Catholics. Well, see, they had really not known that religious preference didn't matter.

The Catholic population was so small they met in a garage. Yes, it was a little garage in back of Mrs. Ford's house. And there was a priest there and we had mass every day. We always had it in the hospital chapel during the week and then met there on Sunday. But, people come to mass every day now. We usually have about fifteen. Some of our doctors and employees. Then the ministers started coming. We started having ministers on call.

Morehead was very different back then. Yes, it was. Coming from Cincinnati and Covington to just one street. See, the shopping centers weren't there. Now there's something like about thirty-five and forty restaurants. At the time there was one, down on Main Street. That was the Eagle's Nest. We didn't go there. We didn't eat out at that time. But every once in a while we'd take a little walk and the people would come out and talk to us. They'd want to know, "How far along is the hospital? Are you really going to open July 1?" We were still in habit then. We only went out of habit in 1968. You really didn't think of it. Now I wonder how we scrubbed floors in all that. So the town people were pretty friendly and glad to have a hospital.

Oh, yes, and the ministers . . . I don't know now what we would do without them. And, you know, we don't think of them as being another spiritual denomination. You just think of them as all being like one . . . spiritual help. And sometimes a patient will say, like in the emergency room, "Do you have a minister or something?" We'll say yes, and they'll say, "But I'm not Catholic." We say it doesn't matter because we call them all here.

And, like Harold Tackett—he is Dr. Louise's pastor—in charge of their church. I think you would love that guy to death. He is just tremendous. See, when he took his pastoral care—you have to take so many hours— and he took two or three semesters toward pastoral care. You don't have to take them, but you can. Even though he's a minister, he really wouldn't have to. But he took that, and then he took his volunteer hours in the emergency room. He was there for several evenings, from seven to ten. Oh, I missed him so when he wasn't there. He would make up stretchers and be around to take patients in and out and call relatives. He'd take patients to the floor or go over in X ray and check them just to see how they're doing. They were simple things, but still it was something that I would have had to be doing. Really, like a real upset mother with a real sick kid or someone, you see, that the doctor would have to say to, "This is terminal. It won't get any better." There was Harold! Right there. That emergency ward gets hard at times.

When I first met Louise, I was about twenty-eight. So that was thirty years ago and she would have been fifty. I was struck by her right away. Oh, yes, as soon as you see the woman, there is something about her that you fall in love with her. I thought she was much younger than she was because of her energy. And you can tell right away. Why, every night Susie and she would come through the hospital after they left the office. Come to the hospital to see how far it was the men got. And I think that's what got the men going so fast that they really worked harder and got things finished so that they were ready to open by July 1. Now, we'd come here on April 2, and the first baby was born here—I can get it for you here in this book we keep. The first baby was born at July 2, 3:31 on Tuesday. His name was Phillip Robert Perkins, son of Mr. and Mrs. Robert Perkins of Morehead. Dr. Billie Jo Caudill was the doctor. The new arrival weighed 8 lb. and 2.5 oz.

This book is what we call our annals. We write down all the interesting things. And the first death was Grace Ford, July 14. Dr. Warren Proudfoot was the first surgeon to arrive—August 1. The auxiliary was started on the sixteenth by Dr. Louise. She was instrumental in that. Now the auxiliary are all ladies and volunteers, and they come and do all kinds of things. Right now the gift shop is closed, but they run the gift shop and then, every month, no, two months, they have what they call a memorial service for the families of everybody who has died. And the families come back and it has really been helpful for some families who have been scared to come back into the hospital since their loved one has died there. And then afterwards they have a little luncheon. Some say, "I never want to see that hospital again." Somehow they say that, and when they get the invitation, they just get the feeling to go back.

This book is just our records. It just says about our arrival on the second of April: "Soon thereafter, Dr. Louise and Susie, her faithful nurse, came to welcome us. The ladies of the parish graciously provided one meal a day in our first days. They also provided transportation to and from church."

Then it records about the different times that the other Sisters came. Oh, the first Sunday after we arrived, Dr. Louise decided we should do something different. She took us over to Bellefonte Hospital [Our Lady of Bellefonte Hospital in Ashland] and we met the Sisters there. And we knew we had to be back for our six o'clock meal, and Dr. Louise put her gloves in front of her speedometer so we couldn't see the rate she was going to get us through those hills to get us back. The interstate wouldn't have been here then. Oh, no, it was all curves.

And here, on July 23, was our dedication of the building. Monsignor Towell was here, and he went around and did the blessing of the building, and they had a copper box that they put different things in it for a corner stone. I don't know if they'll ever open that up. Things concerning construction. Credits to people who spearheaded the hospital drive and the opening up, and the parishes who were responsible for opening up the hospital and getting us here. It also contained pictures of Monsignor Towell and our Reverend Mother.

Our Reverend Mother is the one in charge throughout the world, like in different countries. She stays in Rome. Right now Sister Mary Joelle, who was the administrator here for thirteen years, was elected six years ago. She is in Rome. She is a tremendous person. I grew up with her. We were in Covington together. When she went to Rome, I said to her, "I'm scared you're not coming back." And she said, "Don't be silly." That was the Sunday before she left and a month later she was elected.

Sister Joelle was here for thirteen years. She was the administrator. Sister Edwin was the administrator from 1963 to 1969. Joelle came in 1969 from Covington and stayed to 1983. In 1983 she was elected to Rome. It is remarkable that someone from Morehead, Kentucky, goes to Rome. In fact, she was back here about six months ago for the big opening we had—the ceremonies for all the people who were donating—for our fund-raising. She happened to be down here on visitation. We had a party. In fact, you know the Citizens' Bank, where they have that sign? Well, Mr. Hutchinson, well, Joelle is his God, I think! He thinks there is nobody like her. And he put up in those bank lights "Welcome Home, Sister Mary Joelle." It was flashing all day.

And Sister Mary Edwin, our first administrator, everyone just loved her. She was very motherly. She was much older than Joelle, but still she just had that motherly touch. And her office was near the emergency room, and she'd hear a kid screaming or a family or something, she'd come out. If she wasn't nursing, she'd start helping. She was an RN. She is now ninety-two years old, and she visits the old people at our nursing home in St. Charles every day.

The other first Sisters were Sister Thomasina and Sister Mary Edwin. Sister Mary Thomasina passed away suddenly. She was here twenty-two years. She had myasthenia gravis, a lung disease. To this day people talk fondly about Thomasina, her energy, her enthusiasm. She wrote all the policies of the hospital. She started the Morehead Nursing Program and wrote all the initial books and everything for them—all the nursing care plans and the procedure book. Her big thing was the procedure book. They might have revised it, but I'll bet they're still using that. But the initial one is still up there.

Well, when I came back from [five years in] Indonesia, Sister Joelle said, "Would you like to go back to Morehead? They need somebody real bad in the emergency room." I said, "Yes, I love the emergency room." If I had to pick between OB/GYN, surgery, and the emergency room, I'd have a hard time because the first ten years I worked strictly surgery. But when I wasn't busy there, I'd always help out with OB and the emergency room. But anytime there was surgery, I was there.

Louise assisted in surgery a lot, but not surgery itself. She had enough to do with her babies and all. But at first Dr. Proudfoot needed somebody, so she did quite a bit of assisting, especially on the C-sections that were her patients. All doctors did at first. Two doctors have to be present, you know, for an operation. She would assist; they would all assist. But Dr. Louise was there, I think, more than anybody.

Dr. Proudfoot was remarkable also. Yes, he was. He was a very dedicated man. But Louise Caudill is a very outstanding and dedicated person. She is constantly giving of self to everybody else. I have never seen Dr. Louise angry or upset. She always knows how to keep her cool. I don't think she's got any anger in her at all. Maybe she works out her frustrations after she goes home—on the tennis court and in the swimming pool. But always, no matter what situation she would be in, there's just this calm little lady.

I think the male doctors look up to her. They respect her a lot because they know she has been here so long and what she doesn't know isn't worth knowing. Or, she admits, she knows where to find it. Like Dr. Proudfoot said once, "An intern saw I was looking up something in a book once and the intern said, 'That's stupid. What are you looking in a book for?' And Dr. Proudfoot said, "A smart person is not one that knows all the answers, but knows where to find them. I'd rather see you look it up and know it rather than flub up."

I'm in charge of all the nurses on evenings. My first five years, it was six days a week. But then when I hit fifty-five, they decided I could ease off. But when I came back I asked, "What do you do with a day off?" See, we lived in the hospital and we had our laundry done and we had our cooking done, so what did you do? Well, now I do cleaning. I do a lot of needlework, make scarves and sweaters. I wax the car. I do volunteer service with Christian Services. I try to go once a month—at the Baptist Church, I go once a month.

And people have confidence in the hospital now. It makes me feel good when they say, "This is our hospital. No way do I want to go down the road for anything. This is my hospital. I worked for it, or my mother worked here." There's too many strings tied to it now. You heard about our national award, didn't you? [The National Rural Health Association named St. Claire Medical Center the outstanding rural practice of 1993.] That was won over I forget how many hundreds of hospitals. Up in the hundreds. Maybe close to seven hundred hospitals were up for this.

One thing I got from Louise mostly was her cool and collected way about doing things. She would come in so calm and just start doing things. And I often thought, oh, I'd like to be like her. Apparently it has rubbed off because our nurses will say to me, "How do you stay so calm and cool and collected?" and I'll say, "Hey, if I'm a sick person and I see a frightened person, well, it's going to make things all worse." Especially children. So you have to stay calm and collected, and I think that's one great virtue I've really copied off of Dr. Louise. Mostly I observed it, but I did say it to her, way in the beginning when we'd had a couple of bad things and she was here.

I remember especially the day of our bus wreck, when we had sixty-four patients come in. That was May 7. [Reading from the annals] "May 7, 1964. School bus tragedy. Near 8:30 a.m. on Ascension Day. The sound of horns came close to our medical center as cars and trucks drove to our emergency entrance. These vehicles brought the victims of a near tragic school bus accident. The bus had been sideswiped by a truck, a coal truck, and the driver lost control of the bus and it fell over a forty-foot embankment."

Do you know that hill as you go out on 32? Just after the shopping center and there's a lumber yard. It was over sideways down there. [Continues reading] "There were sixty-two students on the bus. The following article from the *Morehead News* tells how St. Claire Medical Center responded quickly in the emergency room. 'St. Claire reacted to what could have been a major disaster in the Morehead area which is described this week by Sister Mary Edwin, the administrator of the one-year-old Institute.'" This is her report—a whole page long.

Yes, yes, I was there. We were ready to start surgery at 8 a.m. when the police called and said, "They are calling out everybody to help because there is a school bus overturned." Dr. Proudfoot told me to go to the emergency room and start seeing what I could get ready. Then he woke his patient up and told her she would not have surgery because of this. And the lady was very nice.

[Reading] "Dr. Louise Caudill and Dr. Warren Proudfoot examined patients in the emergency room entrance hall as to the extent of the injury. Those with minor cuts and injuries were taken to the consultation clinic where four surgical teams were set up for the injured students who could be moved more quickly. Those that were more serious were treated in the emergency room and the operating room, and six children were sent on to Lexington. They had open fractures: the bones were sticking out of their legs and their arms. Mrs. Laughlin got the auxiliary over here. She blocked the doors and only called parents in one at a time, because the lobby and the halls were filled with sixty-two children lying all over. By noon, everybody was taken care of initially. The initial things and then all small lacerations were sutured."

Some went to Lexington by private cars and some by what we called "black ambulance service" [the hearse]. It would be just about a two-hour ride. The auxiliary did a tremendous job in trying to keep everybody down and calm. All the children survived. The most striking thing was the bus driver [James Ray Martin] who sat out there hurting—you could just see he was in pain—but he would not let us touch him until every child was taken care of. The doctors all closed their offices in town and came out with their nurses. We've had nothing like that since.

But me? Oh, I'm going to keep on nursing now. As long as I feel as great as I do, I'll be in that emergency room.

Dr. Claire Louise Caudill and Susie Halbleib,
June 23, 1993

By the time of our final interview there was only one more week before I would leave for the Wurlitzer Foundation in Taos, New Mexico, where I would finish transcribing the interviews and write the script. They talked about some early experiences with patients, described their early office, and repeated the story of the first visit by Monsignor Towell. As in all our other interviews, we drifted into many other areas.

The final feeling we all had was that we never can really know another person. But I was armed with stories now and knew that the final playwriting had to begin. Dr. Louise and Susie were interested in the place I was going to in New Mexico and, although this was not on the tape, we discussed the possibility of their coming out to New Mexico at the end of the summer. And that is what happened.

SG: *Today, there are little things I want to ask, to piece together what a day was like, living in your office, delivering babies, people waiting, people who needed to go to Lexington and couldn't make it, etc.* CLC: Yes, and I remember a man coming to the back office door and half his skull was off. You could see his brain! You remember that man, Suz, and his skull all . . . ! SH: Oh, I remember. CLC: We had one, you could see the heart and the lungs working and he was alive! I mean, it was unbelievable what all you would see. Walking, but no, they were usually in a truck or something like that.

SG: *Was this from guns?* CLC: I don't remember what happened to that skull, but the heart and lung had been in a wreck. SH: It was a wreck with five people seriously injured, and I think three of them died. I mean, because we had no hospital. CLC: One little girl was running around and she didn't know beans from apple butter. She had brain injury. But she got all right. SH: Yes, she got all right. It was pitiful. That was on Highway 60, and people were going through town because this was the main highway. CLC: And you couldn't help them. It was so . . . I mean, that's the thing that just cuts you all the way through. Helpless. SH: Well, I had forgotten that letter to Monsignor Towell completely until that fortieth anniversary affair, and I came across it accidentally.

SG: *That letter seemed crucial to me because it must have been something about that letter that got Monsignor Towell to come here.* **SH:** Well, the idea was that he did want to know what we did in a day in the office, but his main question was, how many people do we send out of town. And it was amazing how many.

SG: *Were there a lot who didn't make the trip?* **SH:** Not an awful lot. Oh, then many have died after they got there. We would talk to the doctors in Lexington and tell them they were coming and they would be prepared. We had an awful lot of direct contact with the doctors there. Now we hardly know anybody down there.

SG: *This is also a very picky point, but when Monsignor Towell came to the office and saw these babies, well, I've heard that there were four and then five and also six. You said, there were two sets of twins and a singleton—so there were five?* **CLC:** Now Susie says that isn't right, but I think it is. **SH:** That's all right. We had several babies, but I think they were all singletons. But we did have in one night two sets of twins and a singleton. Not necessarily that time, but we had several babies. We had them on the couch.

SG: *Would you wrap them in blankets and lay them this way or that way? That way meaning with their heads toward the end, in a row like carrots or something.* **SH:** We had only one baby bed. You know, ordinarily, we just had one baby, but frequently we did have more. **CLC:** I know we had one in a drawer one time. **SH:** There wasn't one in a drawer the day he came. I think we kept it in with its mother, in the drawer. That was another time.

SG: *I know that McConkey has that story, and Ellie Reser used that story, and so it's been used, but it is hard to not use it.* **CLC:** But you'd like it to be right.

SG: *Yes, I want it to be right, but to me the real point of that is "fate."* **SH:** Right. It really was fate, and it was amazing how it happened. **CLC:** He came about ten o'clock in the morning. And, oh, that was such a busy time for us. Oh, that office! You know, we had a big waiting room, and by that time of day it was just full! People would come and spend the day. I mean, they'd wait a long, long time. They don't wait like that now. Sometimes they had to wait for a baby to be born. **SH:** Why, I think that little Denise Rayburn, who works in the office now, would absolutely die with the way we used to be, but I think Mary Helen Bland could handle it. You know, we'd have to leave with an office full of people to go to the hospital or, when we delivered in the office, we'd be out of circulation for a couple of hours. **CLC:** Do you remember that time we had that fellow who had polio so bad in that one leg and had broken the other leg and we also had that woman in labor and we couldn't get the ambulance to come? Back then we'd call a funeral home and they would take them someplace. But they wouldn't come and get this man quick enough, and we just had to stay and deliver that baby. So I just picked that man up and carried him out and put him in the car or whatever he'd come in. See, I had to get him out of there because that woman was yelling bloody murder. I just knew I had to go quick. Oh, these stories are interfering with your problems.

SG: *Oh, no. They're helping. When the women were giving birth in your office, what would fathers do?* CLC: Sometimes they'd watch. Sometimes they wanted to get as far away as they could. SH: Most of them stayed away, which we welcomed. CLC: Oh, and then sometimes they'd want to help you.

SG: *Jane told me about when her last child was born, that you and Susie were so tired that you both came over and just got in bed with her, one got in on one side and one on the other side and you both went back to sleep. I'd like to use that to kind of emphasize how fast you were going and how tired you got.* CLC: Yes, that's right. SH: That's right. CLC: And did she tell you that she drank a beer shortly afterwards? We played bridge that night!

SG: *She said that having that baby was fun!* CLC: I believe it was. SH: There was a lot of stress and strain, too. CLC: The first baby I'd ever seen delivered was Jane's. Dr. Parks in Lexington delivered it. Oh, I was grown up then, but it was before I went to med school.

SG: *You just wanted to watch? Did that have anything to do with your med school decision?* CLC: Oh, no, but I thought, oh, if all babies looked like that one, it'd be hell on wheels.

SG: *This next question is for both of you—and rather silly maybe—but have any of your male patients proposed to you?* CLC: [Head in hands.] No, no one has ever proposed to me. Sad.

SG: *Somewhere I read that sometimes men are so trusting or grateful and so they just fall in love with you. Didn't happen? Maybe you were just too busy and didn't recognize it.* CLC: I find that there are a lot of things I didn't recognize at the time.

SG: *Also I asked you about some music.* CLC: I have a list. And as far as a hymn was concerned, I love "How Great Thou Art" and then "The Lord's Prayer." I can give you a whole lot of those. Oh, here's the list. I also like "Impossible Dream." And *Rhapsody in Blue.* Did we put *Bolero* in? That's one of my favorites.

SG: *I also thought of one. Do you know "This Little Light of Mine, I'm Gonna Let It Shine"? A children's song.* **SH:** Oh, yes, I like that, too.

SG: *Then I asked you about any favorite Bible passages.* **CLC:** You know, I don't think it's Bible verses that I really like. I think it's Bible attitudes. You know what I mean?

SG: *You mean, inspiring or consoling?* **CLC:** It doesn't come out in a verse. It comes out in my interpretation of the verse. And that's my songs, too. They are two verses. I believe, "In the beginning." I believe that I use that in my thinking as much as anything. From Genesis, "In the beginning there was the word." I believe that.

SG: *You mean, like start at the top and just go where you have to go next?* **CLC:** No, I just believe "In the beginning" is an important thing—and then deciding how things go. Seems like the Bible says that—"In the beginning." I think that's where things ought to be.

SG: *How do you apply that to, say, working with sick people?* **CLC:** Well, you just begin in the beginning, how were they, what happened, how did this get out of whack, and how did that get out of whack. And it just seems to me like that is just sort of a big part of all of life.

SG: *Like, to get somewhere, you have to start somewhere?* **CLC:** And "In the beginning" is where everything starts.

SG: *Now, Sister Jeanne Frances was talking about Sister Joelle, and she said that Sister Joelle gave this wonderful speech, and the idea of it sounded wonderful—that Sister Joelle was talking about the spirituality of this town. By that she meant how all the different denominations in this town came together to support them [for the hospital] and worked together. I was wondering if you heard that speech?* **CLC:** We talked it over, Sister Joelle and I both, about what we were going to say.

SG: *So here is a town that is somewhat factionalized, and in come the Catholic sisters, and instead of everything falling apart, it all came together. For example, the ministers of all denominations came to work in the emergency ward and that was a kind of spirituality of this town.* **CLC:** Yes, it is surprising because almost all of the ministers in this town are a part of the ministerial association in the hospital. That's really something. There was some little strife to begin with, but it ended.

SG: *Were you the one who brought Dr. Proudfoot here?* **SH:** He was going to leave Pikeville. **CLC:** I know he came down to the office and it didn't take him long to make up his mind. He came down one day and called the next morning before breakfast saying he'd come. It was just that quick!

SG: *And he started the Cave Run Clinic?* **CLC:** Well, they all started out as one group. The original idea was that the hospital would hire all the doctors. That was the philosophy of the hospital in the beginning. But I would say surgery and medicine had a disagreement. A difference in the attitude of their profession. First they had this little bitty house and it wasn't big enough for all of them, so what they decided was that surgery would go one way and medicine would go the other. So that's what happened. He built the one on the hill, and Dr. Carpenter and Dr. Black built the Morehead Clinic. Dr. Proudfoot served a definite purpose here, wouldn't you say that was true? **SH:** Yes, and he helped get surgery residents here. We had medical residents, but we didn't have surgery residents. And part of that was because the head of surgery changed down there, too. But he was the one . . . . I suppose his name ought to come up because he was the first surgeon. Then a Mrs. Ford, who gave the land, who wanted to be the first patient admitted. She was admitted, but she wasn't the first patient. Flora Gully was the first. **CLC:** She was my patient. Well, in the beginning most of the people were my patients. **SH:** Wait, now, Mrs. Ford did not give that land for the hospital. That's a misunderstanding. **CLC:** She gave the land for the church.

SG: *Oh, I thought she'd given the land for the hospital. Who did the land come from?* **CLC:** It was Uncle Sam's. **SH:** Uncle Sam owned it.

SG: *Wait, you mean the United States of America Uncle Sam, or your Uncle Sam?* **CLC:** My Uncle Sam. He didn't give it to us. We bought the land.

SG: *Another question. Did you two just never need much sleep?* **CLC:** I need it now, but used to be I could get by pretty easy. I mean, you can sort of get into the habit of not sleeping, I think. Like, when we were working all night, we just couldn't sleep. I might curl up in the back of the car for a while. But we just didn't get the opportunity to go in and go to bed. **SH:** You just make yourself go. And sometimes we'd go away. **CLC:** Sometimes we'd just get on a plane and go to, oh, Africa. So we saw an awful lot of the world at that time. We'd go to New York. We used to see plays. Now, they tell a good one on me. We got into New York one time to see Katharine Cornell in *The Barretts of Wimpole Street*. Well, it just got so awful comfortable sitting there that all of a sudden I went to sleep and snored out loud! **SH:** Yes, with Katharine Cornell walking back and forth and we were right up front!

SG: *I was thinking, even after all this interviewing, can we ever really know another person? I mean, you know each other well, but do you* *ever really know another person?* **SH**: No, I don't think so. **CLC**: There's a lot about Susie I don't know.

SG: *I'm realizing that it is an impossible thing and maybe that's the whole theme. That maybe you don't even really know yourself.* **CLC**: I think that's true, too. We're a different person from time to time.

SG: *And we're often different people* with *different people.* **CLC**: Yes. The audience makes the difference.

Me 'n Susie
A profile of
Dr. Claire Louise Caudill
of Morehead, Kentucky

A PLAY IN TWO ACTS FOR ONE PERFORMER

BY SHIRLEY GISH

Preface

I wrote the playscript for *Me 'n Susie* during the summer of 1993 while on a residency fellowship at the Helene Wurlitzer Foundation of Taos, New Mexico. In May 1993, the president of Morehead State University, Dr. Ronald Eaglin, heard about what I was working on. He called me into his office and said the university would like to give this play its premiere performance. He even had a date picked out for the performance in Button Auditorium: November 12. He saw this work as a fine salute to Dr. Caudill and to the Morehead community.

When I told him that he was arranging for a play that had not even been written, he did not seem disturbed. *I* was disturbed. How, I wondered, could I glean what I wanted from these hundreds of pages of interviews when some of the interviews had not even been transcribed? Then there had to be time to memorize, rehearse, and stage the play. It did not seem possible to do all that in such a brief period. Fortunately, I was able to hide away at the Wurlitzer Foundation for two and a half months.

There were so many wonderful stories and so many decisions to make about what had to be in the play and what, given a play's two-hour time limit, could not get in. I was fortunate to have Travis Lockhart, head of the Morehead theatre department, as the director. He read and commented on various drafts that I mailed to him. That summer is still a blur of papers and small miracles.

By the end of August, I had a working script. But then came the biggest hurdle of all: the reaction of Dr. Caudill and Susie Halbleib. After all, it would be their lives up on that stage. Those intrepid women came all the way to Taos to make a "house call" on me. One dark-blue New Mexico evening they sat and listened as I read it to them. Then I went out into a courtyard so they could talk. Susie was crying. Dr. Louise came out and hugged me and said, "How could you do so much with so little?" Then we both cried.

Arriving back in Morehead, I had to begin perfecting the script and, once again, Travis Lockhart was indispensable. Dr. Louise truly went above and beyond the call for interview cooperation by helping us with the performance details. For example, she spent a Saturday morning showing me how a breech birth is delivered, using her toy bunny as the baby. On stage this was done with hand movements only, but they had to be correct. Also, I was to serve a tennis ball in one scene. Dr. Louise worked with me on her courts on Wednesday afternoons showing me exactly how to do a strong solid tennis serve. She wore me out.

At this point set designer William J. Layne became involved. It was September and we were faced with having to mount a full-fledged production by November.

The playscript published here is a shorter version of that first script, for as with any script, there is constant revision. It should be read as the record of one performance, given at the Lexington (Kentucky) Opera House in June 1994. The stage directions, set, and lighting cues are set down as they were done in that performance. Another director, scene designer, and actor might well see this script produced in an entirely different manner. Often a playscript is seen as simply a blueprint for a director. Reading a play is unlike reading a story. Meanings and feelings are left to be demonstrated by the actor through the vision of the director. Also unlike a story, a play usually has the constraint of a specific time period, usually one hour and forty-five minutes. As this script was written for only one actor, there was the further difficulty of keeping audience attention for even that length of time.

As director, Dr. Travis Preston Lockhart was in the unusual position of knowing not only the playwright and actor but the subjects. In addition, he knew of no other script about living persons. His vision for this script was to portray Dr. Louise as a storyteller, as someone who loves people and always talks and listens directly to people. He felt that the force of her personality and the impact of her life would be overshadowed by elaborate scenery and costumes and props.

In keeping with this vision, Dr. William Layne designed a large playing space to facilitate a lot of movement by the actor. A thrust stage was built to do away with the separation from the audience of the traditional proscenium stage. Dr. Layne painted a giant scrim for the back of the stage depicting the hills and forest surrounding the town of Morehead. Taking a cue from Dr. Louise's sister Lucille's description of her, as a tree with many branches reaching out to people, Dr. Layne constructed a huge tree at center stage.

Props and sound effects were equally minimal, and actual props were used only when they could not be effectively pantomimed. Thus the breech birth was done with hands only, while the tennis serve required a real racquet and balls. Sound effects were used only to add to a scene or show a time change.

The play as directed kept me, the actor, in almost constant movement, since Dr. Louise was seen as very athletic and active, despite being over eighty. Wearing traditional medical whites was seen as too limiting, so sports clothing in shades of deep rose and tennis shoes were worn in both acts. Short hair and comfortable clothes and shoes facilitated movement.

The published version of this play should be understood as an example of the kind of creative work that can be drawn from traditional oral history—the translation of oral history into another living genre.

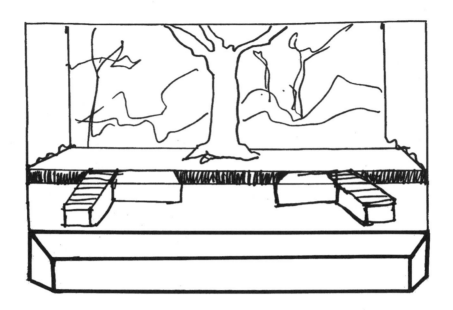

Me 'n Susie

PRE-SHOW MUSIC: "'Tis a Gift to Be Simple"

SETTING: *The stage arrangement is the same throughout. The set was designed as an overall playing space with a thrust stage. The center well (down a step) was used, along with lighting changes, for changes of scene. Four six-foot benches were arranged in L-shapes, right and left of the center playing space were used for other actions. A scrim at back shows the landscape, trees, and hills of Morehead. A huge tree stands upstage center.*

CAST. *Dr. Louise is barely five feet tall. At the time of this play (1993) she is 81 years old. She has been an athlete, and this is evident in her walk and stance and other movements—quick and strong. She uses her wide smile as if it were words. Her hands and arms are either in constant motion or in her pockets. She sits with legs apart and hands clasped between them or on her knees. She has short, white, practical hair and dresses comfortably. In this performance, a deep rose sweatsuit and tennis shoes were the costume. For the second act a fucshia silk pantsuit with a white blouse was worn.*

Act One

PROPS:

> *A three-page folded letter*
> *A cigarette, a lighter, and an ashtray*
> *A tennis racket and three balls*
> *A news clipping in her pocket*
> *A large medical book*

LIGHTS UP *on a huge tree at center stage. Sitting in the branches is a little girl. She is laughing and having great fun.*

OFFSTAGE WOMAN'S VOICE: Claire Louise Caudill! (*Voice gets louder—calling and impatient*) Oh, Claire Louise Caudill! You come home right now!

OFFSTAGE MALE VOICE: Louise. Oh, Louise, we are waiting. Louise.

OFFSTAGE CHILD'S VOICE: Weezer. Hey, Weezer! C'mon, Weezer!

CHILD *climbs down from the tree and does cartwheels off the stage. From behind the tree trunk enters the adult LOUISE. Smiling, she comes forward and sits down close to the audience.*

"In the beginning . . . . In the beginning God created the heavens and the earth." You know, I can't really say that I have a favorite Bible verse. What I guess I've got are favorite Bible parts—some parts and what sense I get out of them for living. "In the beginning" just about says it all for me. Everything has to begin somewhere and then you do the next thing and the next thing.

In the beginning, we are born, All of us started out exactly the same way. As a doctor, I guess I've seen something, oh, about eight thousand or more beginnings. Me 'n Susie, that is. About two thousand right in homes and cabins out in the mountains in and around Rowan County.

Susie—that's Susie Halbleib—my nurse and friend, has been right there from the first one. Haven't delivered any babies now for about eleven years. Quit that when I turned seventy. Guess that makes me eighty-one. But I never got tired of it. Every birth is like a miracle. At first, you know, they just lie there, doing nothing, all scrunched up like this, and then all of a sudden those eyes just open up and boop! There you are.

Your beginning was a miracle, and so was mine. For me it was a miracle to be born in Morehead, Kentucky, into the kind of family I had. I've been lucky, and life's been good to me. Sometimes when they give me awards and honors 'n doctorates 'n stuff, I just wonder, what's all this fuss about? I just did what I had to do, and the next thing and the next, and I was very lucky. It was a lot of hard work, and it was fun.

LIGHTS UP *on the whole stage. Backdrop is a view of the hills and town of Morehead. In the foreground is a space representing the Caudill family cemetery.*

And here was my beginning, in the Caudill family cemetery. My whole family is here. Or will be. Over there is Morehead, where I was born on August 19, 1912. Eastern Kentucky.

You know, it just riles me something terrible when I hear people talking and writing about us in these Kentucky hills being backward and, well, just plain ignorant. I hate that. I really do. That's why I loved James

McConkey's book *Rowan's Progress*. He sees us as people tryin' to get better—and we are and we have.

It's beautiful here. I like to come up here and just think and look. Look over at those hills. They move. You know, at the end of a day you can see them moving slowly like soft waves. I like to bring people up here. Someone asked me once, "Louise, what do you think of up here?" Guess they thought I was going to say something real deep and philosophical about life and eternity. And I said, "Ha, I just think Grandpa Caudill was one pretty smart man to buy this hill!"

(Pantomines reading from tombstone) My grandpa, Abel Caudill, born 1843, Letcher County. He fought on the Confederate side. Grandpa was a farmer, and he cleared all that land over there in Clearfield. But he was a man who believed in education.

And here's Grandma Caudill—Mary Ann Hall, 1849. There was some woman! Married at eighteen, she had five children by the age of twenty-one. There's this story they tell on her: Seems Grandpa Caudill came in one day from being out grubbing— you know what that is—that's clearing bushes 'n weeds 'n stuff so you can grow things. So he'd been working hard, and there was Grandma up in bed with the second set of twins. Grandpa leaned his hoe up against the wall, looked over at Grandma and said, "Oh, I don't see how I'll ever take care of you and these five children."

Well, Mary Ann—Granny—just rares back in the middle of that bed and says, "Why, Abel Caudill, I can take care of these five children and myself, so surely to the Lord you can take care of yourself!" So they had ten more. All of 'em buried up here.

(Walks center, as if reading from the stones) Emma and Lydia and George. William and Daniel Boone (that's my daddy). Joseph and David. Cornelius and Hannah and Watson. And all fifteen grew to be adults. Grandpa gave each of his fifteen children five hundred dollars when they got married, but my Daddy took his money early and went to law school. He was the first man in Morehead to graduate law school. Daddy believed in education, too, and when I said I wanted to be a doctor, he said, "Weezer, you can be anything you want to be—if you really want to work at it." I've been a general practitioner in Morehead, Kentucky, since 1948 and me 'n Susie are still in practice.

When we started here, me 'n Susie, there were three doctors. That was it. Our first office was on the second floor over the poolhall right behind Daddy's office. Then, the university was still a college, only about six hundred students. And the town was only about three thousand. There was no hospital, no clinic, no interstate, no nothin'.

Now, early on, Morehead was just kind of a dot in a muddy road. But it was a midway place between Ashland and Lexington where people would either stop and eat or come to for help. The nearest hospital was in Lexington. Back then it took two and a half hours on a winding road to get there. And we didn't have an ambulance. We used the hearse from the funeral home, and later on we even had to use the dogcatcher's van. We had people that needed a hospital and just couldn't make it that far.

We loved this place and the people in it. All me 'n Susie wanted was for everyone to be well. But right from the start it was pretty clear that you can only do just so much. We knew we needed a hospital here, and that was our goal—to see that we had a good hospital here in Morehead—the absolute best!

It was unbelievable all you would see. And you couldn't help. I remember one night a man coming to the back X-ray room door. Half his skull was blown off. You could see his brain. And we had one man shot. Why, you could see the heart and lungs still working, and he was still alive! I mean, it was amazing all you would see—walking in, sometimes, but usually brought in the back of a truck or something.

Sometimes it was from a wreck. We had this one wreck with five people, and because we couldn't get them to a hospital, three of 'em died. One of the survivors was a little girl who was running around and around and didn't know beans from apple butter because she had a brain injury. She got all right, but it was pitiful. And you couldn't help them. It was so . . . I mean . . . that's the thing you see, when you can't help. It just cuts you all the way through.

We didn't want to see this town stay helpless. Getting a good hospital here—that's about all me 'n Susie talked about while we were driving into the county, going up hollers, on house calls, back in the office over the poolhall, and later on sitting up with women in labor in our little clinic. At first, it was like some kind of impossible dream. Now, once everyone got going with the hospital, it didn't take long. But in the beginning . . . oh, in the beginning . . .

That hospital was always our goal, but it didn't really get under way in a serious way until 1960. And there was some fussing and also a lot of luck. You can also call it grace or divine intervention, whatever you want to call it. And I'd like to tell you this story right up here to start. Now, this happened later, but I'd like to tell it now 'cause it just goes to show how fortune takes care of us.

You see, this is almost entirely a Protestant area. Morehead is in the Bible Belt, I guess you could say. Oh, I guess there were about a dozen

Catholics here, including students, and Susie was one of 'em. They'd meet back in Mrs. Ford's garage. We'd written to every organization and church group you can think of, asking for help in running the hospital—Baptists, Methodists, my own Christian church, Presbyterians—you name it. They all turned us down except Monsignor Towell of the Catholic Archdiocese of Covington. He wrote us and wanted to know how many people we had to send to the hospital in Lexington. It was amazing how many.

LIGHTS *focus on center area; the rest of the stage is dark.* SOUND: *Crying babies and sounds of people talking throughout the scene.*

One morning, at about 10 A.M., right in the middle of the usual riot that went on in our waiting room, in marches Monsignor Towell—unannounced. We had our little clinic by then where we could live, see patients, and also deliver babies. And me 'n Susie had had us some night! Five babies. We had run out of space for 'em, so we wrapped 'em and lined 'em up on our couch—like a little row of carrots.

(Turns, startled) "Monsignor—I, uh, we didn't expect you to just —*(There is a moan from a woman in labor.)*

Excuse me. *(Turns as if to Susie)* Susie, could you stay with Mrs. Brown, please?

(Back as if to Monsignor) "If we'd known— *(Pause)* Well, I guess it is just sort of an average day. *(Pause)* Crying back here? Oh, come look! *(Pause)* No, it wasn't quintuplets. See these first two. Those are the first set. Came just around midnight. And this little girl in the middle here came about 2 A.M. And this little boy and girl, they are twins, too. They came about six this morning. Guess we just sort of ran out of places for 'em. *(Pause)* The mothers? Well, one is in my bed, and one is in Susie's bed, and one is on the X-ray table. Mrs. Brown's on the labor table now, you see.

"All those people in the waiting room? Well, I guess they understand and are used to waiting. They visit with each other a lot. Sometimes they even bring their lunch. *(Pause)* Tonight? Oh, no. If everything is fine, all of these fellas and their mommas will be going home tonight. We can't keep 'em.

"Somebody's got to go pretty soon. I've got a guy out there in a truck with a broken leg. I had to carry him back out there myself. He couldn't stand all the noise in here. *(Pause)* Sure, we can send you sort of an outline of a typical week. Right, as soon as we can. *(Pause)* What's Hill-Burton money? *(Pause)* Government money for hospitals? Well . . ."

LIGHTS *on full stage*

(To the audience) Now I call that divine intervention. And we didn't exactly lie, but we just sort of didn't tell him that we didn't deliver that many babies on a daily basis.

After Monsignor Towell's visit, he'd asked us for a letter. He wanted one week's schedule for our office, but we just sent him one day's schedule that was pretty typical. I'd like to read you a copy of that letter. *(Unfolds a letter to read and lights a cigarette)*

October 17, 1960.

Enclosed you will find an itemized account of a day's office procedure for October 3. Also, a brief description of Morehead and surrounding community in relationship to our need for hospital facilities. We did not do a complete week because of lack of time and also decided it would be a considerable amount of your valuable time to read it. This is, however, pretty typical of most every day.

List for Monday, October 3:

3:00 A.M. Patient admitted in labor.
7:30 Breakfast.
9:00 A.M. Started seeing patients in the office.
    1. Routine prenatal checkup.
    2. 42-year-old woman—post lung resection—cardiac decomp.
9:30 A.M. Admitted woman in labor.
    3. 15-year-old girl—too fat.
    4. 55-year-old woman—hypertension.
    5. 6-week-old infant with pneumonia.
    6. 30-year-old man with gastritis and emotional problems.
    7. 75-year-old woman with infected finger.
    8. 40-year-old woman—vaginitis.
11:30 A.M. Delivered 3:00 A.M. labor admission patient of a pretty
          little girl.
12:00 noon
    9. 45-year-old woman. Complete physical.
    10. 38-year-old man. Upper respiratory infection.
    11. 36-year-old woman—vaginitis.
    12. 6-year-old well baby checkup.
    13. 60-year-old woman. Routine exam.
    14. 4-year-old child. Upper respiratory infection.

15. 34-year-old man. Lacerations on three fingers requiring su
     turing.
16. 30-year-old woman. Routine pelvic and cauterization.
2:00 P.M. Delivered 9:30 A.M. admission of a handsome crying boy.
17. 70-year-old lady. Hypertension.
18. 37-year-old man. Prostatitis.
19. 18-year-old college student. Broken finger.
20. 19-year-old boy, college student, right knee injured—football.
     Fluid aspirated. TBA injection.
21. 4-week-old baby. Feeding problems.
22. 6-month-old baby. Diarrhea and vomiting.
23. 16-year-old girl. Upper respiratory infection.
24. 3-year-old boy. Upper respiratory infection.
25. 75-year-old woman. Cystitis.
26. 26-year-old woman. Prenatal checkup.
27. Routine prenatal.
28. 60-year-old woman. Diabetes.
29. 55-year-old woman. Car wreck four days ago. Sutures re-
     moved.
30. 28-year-old man. Metal burn on foot.
31. 59-year-old man. Fear cancer of the lung.
32. 11 year-old boy. Fight at school. Chin laceration—rock.
33. 17-year-old girl. Upper respiratory infection.
34. 20-year-old girl, college student. Lymph nodes, bad tooth.
35. 13-year-old boy. Tonsilitis.
36. 19-year-old girl. Pregnant, mass in breast, referred to Lexing
     ton. Sutures removed.

Also, fifteen immunizations, three allergy shots, four dressings changed, one house call. Finished at office at 7:55 and then
made house calls.

We wish to express our sincere thanks and gratitude to you
for your excellent cooperation and interest in securing Sisters for
the hospital. We understand that the Notre Dame order is tops.
Respectfully, C. Louise Caudill *(Puts out cigarette)*

I believe that in the beginning it was not having enough space for
those babies that helped us get a hospital, and later it was the children
who brought us all together behind it.
Now, way back in the beginning, Morehead had a hard time getting

together with all the feuding that went on. In fact, this county was almost shut down. Oh, there's some Tollivers in our cemetery. Momma was kin to them. Yeah, the feudin' Martins and Tollivers. Some folks seem to like that bad part of our history here—they do. It's the nature of us, I guess. You have to have the good side and the bad side. Seems, for the world, that bad side is more interesting. Happy people don't seem to make history. As little girls, Lucille and I saw the last of that feud. We saw Cate Tolliver get shot down on Main Street. We were so little we could barely see out of the window of Daddy's office in the courthouse.

Lucille is the oldest of us children. My parents had five children: two boys and two girls and me. Momma, Rosetta Proctor, ran everything in the house, and Daddy ran everything outside of it.

Daddy was a Democrat and thought everything should be Democratic—in the house and in the world, too. At one point, I even did some time as chairman of the Democratic party here. But when he was elected circuit court judge, he won as a Republican! Have a newspaper article about that. I'd enjoy reading it to you. He was fifty-three when this happened. This was in the newspaper: *(Takes news clipping from pocket)*

Judge Prewitt was without opposition for renomination this year until the last day for filing. Mr. Caudill had told Judge Prewitt he would not run. Mr. Caudill was at Frenchburg . . . .

He had a dispute with one of Judge Prewitt's adherents who knocked him down on the street. Infuriated, Mr. Caudill returned to Morehead and filed for both Democratic and Republican nominations. His messenger reached Frankfort in the last hour for filing.

Only Mr. Caudill filed for the Republican nomination and he carried all four counties.

Daddy was a lawyer and also a banker, but spent most of his time as a judge. So he didn't talk much. He listened. I think I got that from him. I believe I listen pretty good.

My daddy believed in education for all of his children. Momma thought girls should mainly be ladies, but she believed like Daddy about education, too, even for girls. Now, as far as education, I never thought I was smart, so I studied hard.

Bob Bishop, who ran the drugstore here for so long, he's been my best friend since we were six and seven. We studied together all the time, and we were in a dead heat to be first. So I was high school valedictorian and he was salutatorian. There were nine in our class. We were on the debate team together. And, oh, later in my life I really regretted that I couldn't do better at sayin' my speeches.

I was really good at sports, though. Tennis is my passion in life, but, boy, I could sure play basketball then, too! Of course, Momma didn't think girls should be playing basketball. Once I was watching our team play over in Morgan County, and we were losing, and, well—the coach came over to me at halftime and said, "Louise, if we could put you in the second half, we could win." I really hated to go against Momma, but—

LIGHTS *focus on center stage*

(To Momma) "Sorry to be late, Momma. The game went into overtime. *(Pause)* No, we didn't lose. Who told you that? *(Pause)* Well, she left early, because we won in the second half. How? Uh, they put some new people in the game, Momma. *(Pause)* Uh, well, it was—kinda me. *(Pause)* Oh, I'm sorry, Momma. I know. I know it's not ladylike, but Momma! *(Pause)* Well, I borrowed some knickers when the coach came over and said, 'Louise, we could win if we had you in that game.' I didn't really want to go against you, Momma, but they needed me."

(To audience) I loved my Momma. I did.

In our years of delivering babies, me 'n Susie, we only lost one mother. That really hurt us, too. I always thought of my own momma. Momma lived to be ninety-one, and I still remember the day she died. That's about the only time I think I've ever heard Susie talk that way to anyone on the phone and just hang up.

She said, "Oh, this man wants you to come right over to their house because his mother's sick. Momma just died, Louise. You can't make a house call now. I yelled at him because he got so mean. I didn't tell him why. I just said no." Well, we went there. Figured I couldn't do anything for my own momma.

We grew up in a big house on Wilson Avenue. We had fun here. We worked hard, and we played hard. And we were expected to. Lucille was three years older than I was, and Boone was three years younger. Then came "Bud" after six years, and after that came Patty. They were just too young to play with.

While Momma took care of them, Lucille got stuck with me and little Boone most of the time. Now, Lucille was pretty, and she could sing and act, and she just loved to do her shows on the upstairs back porch. She didn't much like having Boone and me being follow cats right behind her. But Momma told us to always follow her, and so we did.

I already told you Bob Bishop was my best friend. We had fun as little kids. This was a great place to grow up. When we were tryin' to persuade those top dog doctors to come to Morehead, we used that as a selling point, and I still believe it.

We all mostly played over at the Evanses' house, because their house was the biggest. We liked to ride up and down on their dumbwaiter. Then, over there, behind Holbrook's Drugstore, that's where we had our circuses like all kids have. We had 'em back there because the boy that lived back there was so good with snakes. Oh, he could do anything with 'em. He was a real outlaw. He gave me a cameo ring once, so I thought he was great. Jewelry always was my weakness. Still is.

My part in the circus was to do flips and tricks like that. Why, when I did my flips at hoedowns, people would throw me quarters. Big money!

Over there, on Main Street, that's where Sidney Evans 'n me would have our lemonade stand. Cille helped some, too. We were maybe seven or eight or something, and we sold lemonade and mud pies. Put real cherries on them, too. We had a lot of satisfied customers. By the end of the day we'd have us quite a few pennies and nickels and dimes. We thought we had all kinds of money!

So we got this idea. There was a little girl living way up in those hills, behind where the university is now. She didn't have much, so we thought she needed a warm winter coat and some shoes. So we sent off to Sears Roebuck to buy them. Of course, we didn't have as much money as we thought, so Momma had to help us out. That package came, so we went up and left her package on the step and ran and ran. Guess we went the wrong way 'cuz we got lost. Once we even got it into our heads to plant zinnias on the street down by the railroad—and we did.

Guess for those folks who've lived in Morehead, I've at least got to mention the famous pony story while I'm at it. That pony's name was Betsy Ross and, oh, what a life that poor thing led. She belonged to the Evanses. Sometimes five of us would try to ride her at once and that pony would just wiggle us off and then take off for her barn in the pasture. See, we all had pasture land then to keep our cow on. That's how we got our milk. Yeah, and most of us had outhouses then, too. Anyway, Drew Evans came up with the idea to take the pony up to their third floor window and stick its head out. That's the way the story goes now, I guess, that there was that pony with its head out the window. Way I remember it, the pony wouldn't cooperate at all when we got it up there. So we took it to the second floor and tried to put it in the bathtub. That didn't work, either. Poor Betsy Ross.

Growin' up here was idyllic. I don't think kids grow up like that anymore. I'd have to say my only problem back then was trying to be the ladylike little girl that my mother wanted. Daddy would always say, "Now, I've got three mighty pretty girls here, but none of them are as pretty as their mother." And she was. She was little and delicate and pretty, and she tried to fix us up like that, too. She'd get us all prissed up for visiting or Sunday school.

We went to the Christian church, Disciples of Christ. That's my church, and I still go there. Why, my granddaddy just knew that if you didn't go to that particular church, you'd wind up in hell for certain. Momma would have matching dresses made for me and Lucille. Different colors but the same dress. Lucille would look so pretty. And I'd look like a cowboy! (*Walks like a tomboy*)

I guess about the whole town knew my Momma. She was always helping somebody. I think some of my feelings about people came from her. I would like to clear up here some talk about my mother, though. The talk around town about her driving is, I believe, highly exaggerated. She'd just hit stuff sometimes. She never hurt anyone. She bought herself that big Cadillac. She had to sit on cushions to see. Besides, Wilson Avenue is pretty narrow, anyway.

By the time I got out of high school, I knew Daddy expected us to go to college. Lucille had already been to several by that time. So, still the follow cat, I followed her up to Ohio State. I thought you went to college to have fun and see the world before settling down. I mean, I didn't have the sense to know you went to college to learn how to make a living. Of course, I was only seventeen years old.

I thought I wanted to be a doctor, but something just wasn't connecting. Now, Susie always knew she wanted to be a nurse. She is a big city girl from Louisville. She went to nursing school there. Her only ambition was to serve in rural health. Why, she even used to dress her dolls up like little nurses. As a kid, they tell me, Susie loved to bandage anything that appeared to be broken. She once bandaged the leg of a dining room table!

And Lucille always had the acting bug. I think since she saw her first Chautauqua show that came here to Morehead. She always knew what she wanted to do, and she did it. She became a teacher. Started the drama program at MSU. Now, Momma thought being a teacher was an acceptable job for a woman.

I knew what I wanted to do—become a doctor—but I guess I just didn't have any sense in my head to know what I was doing. Maybe I was scared that I couldn't really become a doctor. Or maybe I thought I wasn't smart enough. It was in college at Ohio State that I found out how smart I was.

I went to see Lucille in a musical comedy one night. Lucille was so talented. She could sing like an angel and act. And, anyway, this woman was sitting next to me.

(Acts as both voices) "Oh, you're Lucille Caudill's little sister, aren't you?"
"Yes, ma'am, my name's Claire Louise."
"Do you act?"
"No, ma'am, I can't act at all."
"Well, you must sing, too."
"No, ma'am, I can't sing a note."
"Well, you just can't do anything, can you?"

(Addresses audience) Then, in college, they came along and said I had to major in something. Sorry, but it would just be hard to even imagine a more ignorant college student than I was. I couldn't even figure out a major. Well, one night . . .

Sits at table and begins to write a letter. There is a sound of a ball hitting the wall.
"Dear Daddy:
    "I guess this college life is going to be fine. Cille and the others went to a party, but I didn't feel like going. They got all dressed up, and I just wanted to stay in my dorm room. The rooms are nice. There are four of us here. The classes are much harder here, and I'm not sure why I'm even in the classes I'm in. My adviser here says I have to major in something. I don't know what to do."

(A tennis ball comes bouncing from offstage. She looks over at what should be another room.) "What are you doing in there? *(Pause)* A speech? You're practicing a demonstration speech? Then what's all that noise about? *(Pause)* Your speech is about how to serve a tennis ball? Hey, do you have a major? *(Pause)* Physical education? You can major in that? Here, let me show you how to do that." *(Picks up a racket and does a hard serve into wing at stage left)*

(To audience) So, that's how I found my major in college. Serving a tennis ball.
    After college, I just don't know what was in my head about being a doctor. I do know that right after graduation I just got rid of all those books, tossed 'em over. That was enough! That was on June 27. Ha! By July 4 I was on my follow cat way up to New York City. Cille and everybody were going up there to Columbia University. I registered and said

my master's degree would be in physical education. Oh, New York was fun, and I was just busy taking it all in. Then, back at Morehead they needed somebody in the PE department to teach, and it was swimming and tennis and basketball, and so I did that. Went to Columbia in the summers and finished up the degree.

So, for near seven years I taught physical education at Morehead State. It was fun. Well, this is a hard thing to admit: I thought a very bad thing about teaching while I was teaching. Now, I admire good teachers and how important it is to be one. I even did some time on the Council for Higher Education. But teaching just didn't make me feel right. That's not from intelligence. It's something with feelings. It's those daggone emotions you've got to listen to. I had to come clean with myself, because I also know that it's just plain not right to teach when you really are waiting or wanting to be something else. Teaching should be done for itself, not second best, or done in place of something else.

Really, physical education is a pretty good start for medical studies. You have to know anatomy, muscles, nerves, and physiology. Oh, I guess that I wasn't using it as a stepping stone to anything exactly. For me, it was kind of a detour—maybe a deviation. There I was, thirty years old and all around me people were settled into what they were doing. And I was still playing at my games and just thinking about med school. Daddy kept saying, "You can be anything you want to be if you are willing to work for it." And I thought, I'm not a follow cat. I'm a fraidy cat. And I was.

I started having nightmares, like in those doctor movies, and I'd be in that big amphitheater watching bloody operations. Oh, I had awful dreams. But it was 1943—and it was then or never.

I went to talk to my cousin, Dr. Everett Blair. He had an awful lot to say. He told me that being a doctor would simply be too hard work for a woman. I told him that it may be hard work, but I just wasn't scared of that at all. So he said, "Go to a big city to practice after you're done with med school." He told me not to be a general practitioner. Everett said that being a general practitioner would just wear a person out. He told me to not even try to be a doctor. Guess I don't always listen as good as I like to think I do. I did everything he told me not to do.

Finally I was determined to do it. I can't say that made me any the less scared. Oh, I was. I went to Louisville to medical school, and it was during World War II. We were put on accelerated studies because there was a shortage of doctors. I went through in three and a half years, and it was hard. By the way, that's when I took up smoking.

Now, Susie hates smoking. It's even above her pet topic of good nutrition. I smoked for about thirty-five years—and I mean I smoked! I didn't do that polite little light one, take a puff, and put it in the ashtray. I'd take a deep drag and get it way down like this. Someone asked me how much I smoked. I smoked all the time I was awake. I smoked in my office. Oh, I don't know how anyone could stand me. I must have smelled like a sewer pipe. Hardest battle I ever fought was quitting.

Then I went up to Philadelphia to do my internship. I guess most medical students go through some queasy times in the stomach. The first time we had to open up cadavers, well, four of the fellows left. Yeah, I wanted to skeedaddle, too. But by that time I just knew I had to stick it out, and I made it. In Philadelphia, I met the first woman doctor who really inspired me: Dr. Wai Mai Chen, who is now head of obstetrics in Shanghai, China. We're still friends.

After the internship it was time to go out on my own. I was teetotally scairt. See, you're doing all these things in the hospital with other people, but then you think—oh, you've got to do it all by yourself later on. There's going to be nobody else but you. The thought scares you. And only you can know what to do when something unexpected happens. I just figured that most of my practice was going to be in obstetrics, delivering babies, and along came this woman doctor who was head of a maternity center down in Clay County, Kentucky—the Oneida Maternity Hospital. She said she needed some help and kinda promised to teach me all the big stuff. That's what I needed.

So in the winter of 1947 I went to Clay County. Clay, huh? Mud was more like it. I think their leading product there was mud. There were four nurses there and a nutritionist. Right off I was in charge, and the lady doctor simply disappeared. Lucky for me those nurses knew their stuff. And the most self-confident one was Susie Halbleib.

Now, Susie was so calm and—as she says now herself—she sure knew everything there was to know at twenty-one. Susie believed that as long as she was sitting by a mother in labor, nothing could possibly go wrong. Nothing did, either. She just sort of seemed to know what to do.

Me, I always had to run to a book to check stuff and see what all I didn't know. I still do that, too. But here I was the doctor, and I was supposed to be in charge. That's when I grew up.

One night we got this call at Oneida that a woman was being brought from Redbird and she was in trouble. Evidently she had had the baby, but the placenta was not coming—the afterbirth—and she was in pain and bleeding and all. Her whole family was coming in with her in a wagon.

(Runs for a book and sits on the floor) I don't know any more about what to do than a jackrabbit! Oh, I've got to find something before they

get here. I've never had this one before. Got to check. Let's see. *(Gets up)* They're here? All right now. *(Checks back in book, slams it shut)* I guess I got it.

(Looks up as if praying, moving her lips) She's ready? All right, God. Let's do it.

I strode by her whole family trying to look like I knew about confidence. She was up on the table. Susie was sitting there holding her hand, and I went over and, oh, just put my hand on her stomach—gentle—like that. Boom! Out it slides. Susie and I just stared at each other, stunned, I guess. Well, Suz says, matter-of-factly, "Guess it got jogged loose being bumped around on that buggy ride." That's when I grew up—*finally*. I was thirty-five years old. There was nobody to defer to, nobody to ask. Nobody but Susie.

Then the first emergency call came in from out in the county. I just believed I couldn't ignore those. Oh, I couldn't even figure out what to wear. Boots, for sure. Susie was at the door, and she handed me a medical bag and said, "It's all packed. Everything you might need is in here." I didn't even think of that. She's been way ahead of me ever since.

She said, "You have to get to believe in yourself."

I said, "You've also got to have someone who believes in you."

So later I told Susie, "Look, I'm going to Morehead to begin my general practice at the first of the year. I need a nurse, and I'd sure like to have you come with me. The mud's not so bad. There is a college there."

Susie thought it over. Said, well, she'd like to take some art courses at the college, and if a Catholic priest was there for mass, then, well, she'd give it a try for one year. *(Smiles)* And that was forty-five years ago!
CURTAIN

Act Two

SPOT on LOUISE. *She is wearing a sports suit and is holding a tattered toy rabbit as if it were a baby.*

LOUISE: This is bunny. He's a good bunny. You can hug him just any old way. The Sisters at the hospital gave him to me. I can't remember why or when, but I keep him around all the time to hug. I know, people say, "Dr. Louise can make a crying baby stop crying just by touching the baby and holding it!" Now, there's no magic to that. What you need to do is just take that baby and hug it really tight and up against you, see? You take a new mother. They hold that kid like this. Well, it's probably afraid to be dropped. You gotta grab 'em tight.

I think with kids, especially the first ones, you've got to raise 'em in order to know how to raise 'em. Tell you the truth, most babies could probably raise themselves better than most parents do. They know what they need. Why, if they could just get their little hands on that bottle, they could come up without us. But you can't raise good kids without a lot of good hugs.

This bunny's ear is falling off. Has been for a long time. Susie says, "Well, sew it back on." I say, "I don't do sewing." Suz says, "Why, Louise Caudill, if you will think back, you have sewn ears back on two different guys." Now, that's right. Guess I don't see it as the same thing. But we did that. I say *we* because Susie certainly was there and kept her head straight, and theirs, and mine, too! One guy says a horse or a cow bit it off. So I says, "Well, we need to have that ear." So his wife went back and got it, and we sewed it back on. Other guy, I think, had it with him. Some guy bit it off in a bar. Some stuff you just kind of forget.

Like a couple of weeks ago, a fellow comes in to show me his finger. I sewed it on twenty-five years ago, but the people brought him in had it with them, and it grew back perfect. He could move it and it had feeling and even had a growing fingernail. It was like a miracle. I'd forgotten all about that one.

Guess I can just go ahead and fix up bunny here, too.

You know, when I first got out of med school, Bob Bishop asked me,

"Louise, why in the world are you coming back here to Morehead to practice medicine? Of all those places you've been, looks like to me you could pick some other place besides here. There's a lot of disadvantages here."

I said, "Yeah, I know that. There's a lot of problems here. There's a lot of problems everywhere. I'll never find a place there aren't problems." I just decided that if no place was perfect, as far as I was concerned, I might as well come back home and practice where I know the people. Maybe solve some problems.

Before we left Oneida we'd ordered all sorts of stuff: an X-ray machine, sterilizing equipment, and, don't ask me why, but about one hundred years' worth of ammonium chloride tablets. (We still got eighty years' worth somewhere.) We tried to think that we knew what we were doing. Susie and Momma painted and scrubbed up that poolhall office. And there we were ready to open for business.

In the first week we were open for business, Susie and I were leaning out of the window of Daddy's office and Eldon Evans walked by and said, "Hey, what are you doing?" We said, "We're looking for patients."

But after that we were swamped with folks. We'd have so many patients, why, they'd be lined up all the way down the stairs to the street. Me 'n Susie stayed with my parents then—and suddenly there was no time for anything but taking care of patients, house calls, and all. And traveling out into the counties to deliver babies. Can't say I wasn't still kind of unsure.

I remember the first call I got to deliver a baby at someone's house here. Well, Susie had a date and she was at the movies. I grabbed our bags and things and then ran right into that moviehouse and got Susie out. I wasn't going alone! I can't quite remember what happened to Susie's date. Guess we brought him along. Guess it got hard for Susie to have boyfriends.

Then, too, we'd be gone a lot out into the hills. Sometimes for days at a time. Oh, we traveled every possible way into those hills except by helicopter. Usually we'd drive in as far as we could and someone—a neighbor or husband—would meet us and take us on in a wagon or a truck. When the mud was bad, we'd ride on a kind of sled hitched to horses. We got dragged through mud and through snow. And we carried a lot of equipment with us: drapes and IV fluids and a birthing table. We'd be loaded down.

Most places had no water, no electricity. Sometimes other people in the family would be sick, too. Usually we'd never seen the woman before. Most times they couldn't pay, and that was okay. I've never looked at a bill in my life.

Once a man gave us $3.54 for a delivery. That's all they could save up. We said no, but they were proud and we took it. But right from the beginning it was clear that women in this area needed real prenatal care. If there was a problem, we could be in real trouble.

(Removes jacket and pantomimes putting on rubber gloves) Usually now, delivering a baby is just a matter of waiting and watching. We read piles of medical journals waiting for those little fellas to show up, or we'd take naps in the back of our car. Nature really does most of it, but, oh, those little breeches—and I don't mean pants! Breeches—those little fellas that decide to come into the world backwards. Luckily, back then we were taught how to do that. Now they just give a C-section, and I suppose it's easier on all concerned. But for them you really had to wait— and wait. And you'd think, laws, that's it! It's there, just doing nothing and you slide it around, then the little butt rises up and you get a hold of it and you just turn it, turn it around.

(Pantomimes delivering a breech birth) Sometimes a foot is down or two feet are down. If not, you have to go in and turn a leg down and pull it down and hold it . . . go up and get the other one . . . then pull it down and then you pull two of 'em out together . . . then twist around to the shoulders. Go in and first this arm and then cross the cord and then the other arm and then get the cord, hook two fingers into the mouth—take the other hand on the outside and press on the head, then pull and— poof!—there it is. Oh, that's really fun! Oh, to do that is a great thrill! Oh, yeah! It's just like you hit a good clear high note! *(Pantomimes holding baby up with two hands, then sets it down on bench)*

I found out what my cousin Everett meant by hard work. It was. Carrying all that equipment, hiking up hills, going without sleep for days at a time. He was right.

Once we got out to this place—had to hike through a mud field—and the woman had been in premature labor for days and the baby was already dead—just an arm out and we had to get that woman more help than we could give. So, me 'n Susie wrapped her up in some sheets and with one at each end we carried her out. The husband followed us carrying all our equipment. Oh, seemed like miles through a knee-deep mud field. That was a fur piece. I really didn't think I'd make it. We got her into Morehead and into the hearse-ambulance and Susie rode with her to Lexington. They made it okay, too. So it went on and on.

Now, my brother Boone became a lawyer, and he and his wife, Jane, bought the house across the street from my parents, and they had a washing machine. When we'd come back from delivering a baby out in the county, we'd go to Jane's place first—nobody locked doors back then—

and stuff all the drapes and things into her washing machine. Then we'd go down to take care of the lines of people at the office. Yeah, boy, we worked and never got any regular sleep.

Jane decided she'd have her fourth child at home. She thought that would be fun, and it was. She called us at 3 A.M. She thought it was coming. So, me 'n Susie took our stuff right over and then had to wait. We were so tired that night that Susie crawled in bed on one side of Jane and I got in the other side and we just went back to sleep until it was time. At 9 A.M. Jane had a beautiful little girl. Named her Sally.

Yeah, and people would show up at Momma's door at night when there was a real emergency. Guess we were sort of the Morehead night emergency ward.

Once, in the middle of the night, up drives this car from Tennessee. On the way to West Virginia, I think. There's a woman in real labor, her husband, and her parents. That baby was fixin' to get born right then, so we quickly put her in Momma's bed on the first floor. Well, that was all right except that then those people stayed and stayed. We had a time getting them out.

One terrible night there was a pounding on the door and there stood this man and woman holding a small child. That was one sick child. It was vomiting and red around the mouth. Obvious carbon monoxide poisoning. They couldn't understand why this kid was sick when their other two were sound asleep on the floor in the back of the car. (*Nods*) They were dead. Had been for some time.

And, oh, how we hated the summers back then. Polio was so bad. We'd send them to Lexington, but it was usually only two days or so and they'd die. There was nothing we *could* do except concentrate on what we could do. You can't do everything. You can't know everything.

And we had to send people who were so sick so far for specialists. Why, I had to do things in the beginning that I'd never try again. There were times I had to do spinal taps on small babies 'cause there was no time to get them to the hospital in Lexington.

More and more, we realized what we could do was give better prenatal care here. We had to get women to come into town beforehand so they wouldn't get caught later without someone to take care of them.

PHONE RINGS

"What? I mean, what's your name? Uh huh. (*Pause*) She's about to deliver a baby? What's your name and where do you live? (*Pause*) Oh, well, I'll tell you what. I think it would be faster if you drive her in here. And we'll be ready for you. (*Pause*) I know you've never been to us, but you can find us right on Main Street. *(Pause)* Yes, we'll be ready for you. *(Pause)* She's never seen a doctor? Well, we won't scare her. You just hurry on over here."

(To audience) Well, they got here. Woman had never seen a doctor in her life. Thing was, she wasn't even pregnant. Thought she was. He thought so, too. Looked that way, but she was no more pregnant than a door. Now, we could have wasted a whole lot of time going out on a call to people in places we'd never seen. We had to persuade women to come into our office for prenatal checkups. To learn about better diets for the mothers and young girls to have healthier children. There also needed to be checkups and shots for those babies.

Our idea was to build a little clinic, and in 1957 we did that. Then the mothers could come to us. We didn't want one of those awful little lying-in places but a clinic where we could deliver and also take care of our patients. And we lived there, too, so we could stay in and be available. That way, at least one of us could get some sleep!

We got called out for more than just babies. We got called for pneumonia a lot. People here considered anything with a high fever to be pneumonia. Too often we'd be called out for that, but it would be the last stages of cervical cancer. The worst condition we saw back then was cervical cancer. Now you can spot it ahead of time. And they say Pap tests aren't much good. Why, that just burns me up. They just don't realize! When we saw something like a young woman dying of cancer of the cervix, well, it was horrible. Usually somebody isolated way out in the county and lying on dirty sheets. And nobody with them. Never had anything. It just cuts you. And what could we do? We were helpless and they would die and the only thing we didn't know was when. And it came from modesty, and it came from ignorance. I call it ignorant modesty! They would bleed to death. And that's what most of them did—suffer and bleed to death. Young women don't have to do that anymore if they just come in for Pap smears. And after 1957 we had a place so they could do that.

Of course, chicken pox and measles cases stayed at home, and that made sense. Although Susie wonders how many kids actually caught measles in our office. Suz says children shouldn't have measles anymore. In fact, no one should have the measles anymore.

One problem we could never solve and still can't is teenage pregnancy. Our youngest mother was twelve!

We saw an awful lot of children—and we wanted to. I liked the idea of tracking the kids from the time they were born and knowing the whole family. It gives you a better picture, you see. The children, well, *mostly* they loved me, and I loved them all. I wasn't fast enough once and got a good bite on the arm—drew blood!

Now, Susie, she was often the enemy. She gave the shots. We walked into church one Sunday, and a little girl began crying and crying and pointed at Susie and yelled, "Oh, Susie needle!"

Susie was sort of the "enforcer." Had to be. She tried and tried to keep some law and order in that waiting room. Oh, what a commotion that office was. Just a lot of commotion all the time. See, I like to talk to the person, see what all is going on in their life. I do believe I listen pretty good. I just sort of figured it out. Didn't have any course like "Understanding the Patient 404" or anything. By listening you can get a pretty good idea what's goin' wrong. See, you have to get everything together and compare it all. Sort of—well, "in the beginning" and then figure things out. You have to know the whole person—the whole situation. Sometimes, by doing that, they can just look up and tell you what is wrong.

I've heard people tell that I'm a pretty good diagnostician, but I think that's why. It's the whole person involved. It's not the mind or the body. We are one organism. Now they are calling this "holistic medicine." Seems like to me it's common sense. Thing was, according to Susie, I just couldn't do that with all the people waiting. She said I'd see only one patient a day—the first one who came in the door! So she always had to be the bad guy. She had signals like coughs, or banging on the wall, or thumping on the door, and then if I didn't quit, in she'd come!

Now, Ellie Reser is a nurse I admire, and she makes me feel fine to call me a healer. There are many kinds of healers. But I really think one ought to say that about everyone in the medical profession. I know what she means, though. You know, a lot of people go to see a doctor just to talk and be touched and have someone listen. And it is important. Maybe it's the most important part of finding out what is ailing folks. But poor Susie has to put up with my listening habits.

Of course, there were some positives to the way medicine was practiced back in those early days. Some kinds of house calls were one good thing. The patients could stay in their own beds and not get made worse packing 'em into the office. And you could touch people. You could pat and hug people without someone yelling, "Abuse," or some such thing. Touching is so important. It's what healers do. And with old folks, why, me 'n Susie would just drop in for a chat and a smile. Sometimes I'd just get right up in bed with them and we could really have us a little chat, instead of hovering over them and scaring them half silly. The philosophy of living is different now than it was thirty years ago. Now you'd be considered a screwball or gay or abusive or something. Of course, now they think they're discovering the healing powers of touch like it is something new, and they're calling it "psychoneuroimmunology." It's just a friendly pat and a good hug!

Of course, doctors see conditions that we can't stop. Sometimes we can help someone some way. Now, my close friends Norma and Elijah Hogge—I built my house right next to theirs when I could finally build a house—and they lost their daughter to cystic fibrosis, and their little boy Rowe had the same fatal condition. I'll never forget the last time we saw him. He loved to ride his horse. He wanted to ride it in what he called the World's Fair—it was the State Fair in Louisville. He was twelve. They got partway there, but he just couldn't breathe. They brought him back, and we just loaded him up on cortisone and he got to ride in that World's Fair.

Well, sometimes we just plain got tired and we had to get away. And that's how me 'n Susie have seen a lot of the world. Oh, we've been to China and Sweden and Hawaii and Africa, even on a safari. We'd go to New York, because thanks to Cille we loved the theater. I'll never forget the time we got there and right away could get tickets to see Katharine Cornell. I forget in what play. Never even saw it actually. I fell asleep right there in the front row . . . and snored!

And we also kept talking about how we could have a hospital here. A real one. Now, all through the mountains of eastern Kentucky there were little lying-in kinds of places. We didn't want one of those. We'd seen 'em. They were not even hospitals. Many of them were very bad places. One day this fella came through there and wanted to talk to me about putting one of those places here.

LIGHTS *focus on center stage*
(Turns to address man) "You heard right. We do need a hospital in Morehead. *(Pause)* You mean we can have a little hospital here just for deliveries? *(Pause)* Morehead isn't big enough for anything else? Do you think for one minute that is all these people need a hospital for? *(Pause)* We also could make a lot of money doing operations right here? Is that why people do operations—to make money? *(Pause)* Oh, they won't miss an appendix or tonsils or a uterus.

"How dare you! Better than no hospital? I don't believe we have to have a little cheap shoddy place here just because we're a small town. Those places kill more people than cure 'em. I won't have it! OUT! Down the road! Sir, I'd suggest you had better get going right down the road you came in on! *(Pause)* Well, you get my ire up and then, buddy, look out!"

(To audience) Something can just irritate my insides and there may not have been a reason in the world for it. Oh, that man aggravated me—somewhere in here. I go by feelings. I don't go by sense. The idea of one of those awful little places here—and then you're stuck with it.

I said, "Susie! Susie! Get your jacket! We're goin' to start knockin' on some doors. First thing we'll look for—see who'd like to give us what kind of money. We'll get that hospital, and it will be the best one we can get. The best."

(Pantomines banging on a bathroom door) "I don't care if you are in the shower, Eldon. You're the mayor. Open up. I have to talk with you. *(Pause)* Well, I'll just stand by the door and talk to you. *(Pause)* Eldon, I'm your doctor, remember? So here's what we need to know. We want to find out how many people in this town will help us build a hospital. Will they support it? You're the mayor, and I'm starting with you. *(Pause)* No, I'm not going over to Mr. Palmer first. I want you first. Here's a towel.

"Look here, Tick, I'm your doctor. *(Pause)* I know you're in a hurry. *(Pause)* Well, finish dressing, and I'll keep talking in your car while you go to the bank."

LIGHTS *back up on full stage*

(To audience) And we knocked on doors, and others knocked on doors, and we got promises of money and support. And that told us that there was real interest here. Of course, I may have been a little pushy, too. Bob Bishop says I can sell anyone a bill of goods—for no matter what. He says if I'm for something, you just can't figure out enough reason not to do a thing.

And we got up groups of interested citizens and met at the Eagle's Nest Restaurant, where everyone in town went. Even the children helped to raise money. And Snooks Crutcher—he was the editor of the newspaper—he really used the newspaper to get the word out. He was great. And Dr. Doran, up at the university, he was behind us. Said he would give five percent of his salary, and he said that everyone on that campus would do the same thing. So that was the beginning.

And the next thing?

After the facility itself, of course, you had to have people to run it. People experienced in running a hospital—kitchens and records and cleaning, technicians, people who cared about people and were committed to good health care for this area, not just making a profit. And you had to have doctors—surgeons and specialists—because that's what we were really missing here. We didn't want unnecessary surgery and poor medicine—things that can happen so easily in isolated places and rural areas. It had to be planned right. A good hospital has to be more than a fancy building. There must also be a goal and a plan—like people—a body and a soul, too. Of course, somebody committed to running a hospital.

And there's where our luck, or grace, or divine intervention or whatever you want to call it with those babies came in, because the Sisters of Notre Dame agreed to come to Morehead to run our hospital.

I had to give a speech to the hospital committee. Now, we'd gotten the support from our community. But we seemed to hit some kind of a snag. The Sisters of Notre Dame, who are dedicated to poverty and care of the sick, were ready to come here, and I had to get up and tell that to the committee.

(Addresses the committee) "Now maybe you and I don't believe in the pope in Rome, but I can't see where that makes any difference. They will come here to serve us—not to preach and certainly not to ruin this town. Any of you who oppose this plan, please, right now, today, call or write, or both, to your own church headquarters. We guarantee you that we will take any other offer seriously. There are no other offers yet, so please let us unite and give our support to the Sisters. We might just be surprised!"

(To audience) And we were. So the Sisters who gave bunny to me came to Morehead to begin running the hospital in 1963.

Now, we learned from those Sisters. And they didn't have an easy time here at first. At that time they were still wearing the full Catholic nun's habit. Boy, they got an awful lot of strange looks, and people were really suspicious. Why, people would watch them in the grocery store for fear they would try to sneak soup cans under their robes!

But the way they fit in here, why, that's another whole story in itself. Let me say that it was the children that won everyone over to how truly kind and dedicated the Sisters really are. They'd even go out and play baseball with the kids at night.

One of the first Sisters here was Jeanne Frances, and she is still here working in the emergency ward at night. Yeah, there were some problems with religion. Guess we all ought to remember that, back then, in 1960, we weren't the only place asking about Catholics running things. Remember John F. Kennedy running for president? That if a Catholic ran the country, we'd be run by the Pope? That sort of nonsense talk was all over the country.

First week the hospital was open, a fella who was against the Sisters slipped off his front porch. Broke his hip. He thought the Sisters were pretty okay after the fine nursing he got. He was a big enough man to stand up in church, when he could stand up again, and say so, too!

The money and the building and the running of it, that got settled, and we had us a groundbreaking and, oh, the whole town just stopped for that day. It was wonderful. The newspapers had big headlines! The high school band even marched down Main Street!

Next we had to persuade some doctors to come here. Now, we wanted good doctors and specialists here, not just any old "podunk" fellas. Once again, along comes luck or grace or divine intervention—whatever you might like to call it.

At that time I was in a class over in Lexington. Doctors have to keep up, so I would go at night and take classes in their clinic program over there. I was sitting in class next to this nice doctor and started just a-talkin' to him.

(Sits and addresses man) "We're trying to get this hospital going over in Morehead. *(Pause)* Yes, it's two hours away. Oh, but it's beautiful! Has a college there. You ought to come over some time. *(Pause)* Oh, we've got good fishing! So what we are trying to do is get us the better doctors, specialists, lined up for when the building is ready. Do you know of anyone who might be interested? *(Pause)* You do? Who? *(Pause)* You'd be interested? *(Rises and calls after man)* Hey, wait up, we need to talk some more!"

(To audience) The University of Kentucky was just starting a medical school then in 1960. How's that for timing? He knew all sorts of new doctors coming in. His name was Dr. Richard Segnitz and, boy, he became my buddy from then on. Guess we've got to remember that quite often luck isn't out there somewhere. It could be sitting right next to you!

Then the dean of the med school, Dr. Bill Willard, oh, he was a good-un. His philosophy was to send students out to Morehead to see what actually went on in rural health. And Bob Johnson, who was Dr. Willard's right-hand man, helped write grants and recruit doctors, and he kept the peace. Then came Dr. Ed Pellegrino, and his ideas of hospital organization were based on a hospital called Hunterdon up in New Jersey.

I made a speech to the members of the Kentucky Medical Association.

SOUND *of people in an audience talking noisily and disagreeing*
   (Holding a clipboard) Members of the Kentucky Medical Association. There is no doubt in my mind that our plan for the staffing of the new

hospital at Morehead is a good one. We know it will work out the way we have it set up. Each specialist will handle cases referred to them, and they will have offices in the hospital as full-time resident physicians and will teach one day a week in Lexington. Each will have a contract for the same salary per year. All their fees will revert to the Northeast Kentucky Hospital Foundation. I just believe this is a fine plan. I believe it is.

(Slams down the clipboard; addresses audience) Well, I sure bungled that one! Should have paid more attention to how important it is to outline a good persuasive speech. I just knew it would work fine and figured they just ought to have sense enough to know that, too. That was awful. Oh, did I hear about that! Oh, I was a bad girl! They called me a communist— a socialist—I don't know what all. The KMA threatened to disbar me. Yeah, because of having a doctor's office right in the hospital. They said a hospital is a place you *come* to work. Guess they thought it was against free enterprise or something.

Well, about a million things went wrong, but that was the worst. So I went down in defeat, and we moved those guys out, and eventually it turned out just fine. We got two good clinics out of it, Morehead Medical and Cave Run clinics.

Now, this might be a pretty small town, but we were after "top dog" people here. We had to work to attract them. That's when I started to build a house. We wanted to show prospective doctors that they wouldn't come over here and have to live in some kind of primitive log cabin or somethin'. We wined 'em and dined 'em. Well, Susie dined them.

I believe that there's a lot of people, even if they are smart and rich, that would prefer to live in a nice little friendly area rather than alone in a big city. And many did and still do. We sold Morehead as a good place to work and to be, and that goes for the university, too. Quality will attract quality. And the hospital grew and the university grew.

Of course, it was pretty nice to have a house. We'd lived with my parents or with patients since 1948. I was fifty-eight years old. Oh, it was hog heaven!

So we opened that hospital, and they've just dedicated the third addition to it there this year. And for the second year in a row St. Claire Medical Center was named the Outstanding Rural Hospital in the United States.

Saint Claire. Hmmm. Sister Mary Borromeo and a small committee decided on that name for the hospital. They talked about naming it Morehead Medical Center. Then they talked about naming it after St. Francis of Assisi, but he took care of animals. Then Sister came up with the fact that a St. Claire took care of sick people, and so did I, and my first name is Claire. It's peculiar, yes. Saint Claire? Nice, too, the recognition. But Susie never got much recognition. Not one award or honor, and she was right there through everything.[1] Like the supporting actress.

When you come to think about it, see, I was here where I came from and where my family is. Susie gave her whole life to this town and had no real reason to . . . except she just wanted to be a nurse in rural health. And she never got to take an art class! Of course, she did get to bandage an awful lot of broken bones, and all of them on the same day back in 1964, the year the hospital was opened.

It was a terrible day, but also the kind of emergency that showed what this town could do. And we finally all pulled together behind this hospital and thanked God for it. Again, it was children that did it. Religion didn't matter any longer.

PHONE RINGS. *Rest of stage is dark.*

"There's been a what? A crash? Oh, no! Where? *(Pause)* Highway 32, but where? *(Pause)* A school bus? Down the embankment by the lumber yard. Oh, no. No! Do you know how many? Sixty-four! Yes, we'll bring everything we can. Tell 'em we're on our way."

FLASHING LIGHTS, AMBULANCE SIRENS

All those children. Everybody volunteered to do something, and we did it. Dr. Warren Proudfoot became a hero. So did the bus driver, James Ray Martin, whose arms and ribs were broken but who refused treatment 'til all the children were taken care of.

Every minister of every faith was there. No one worried about any other religion, and we all saw the grace of those Sisters under pressure. I don't think this town was ever the same after that. And all of the children survived. A miracle. The hospital now belonged to everyone.

I think that's why Mother Joelle, our former Mother Superior, when she came back to visit from her headquarters in Rome, could call this town a spiritual place. I believe there is a friendship in these mountains that you just aren't going to find anyplace else. I believe that.

LIGHTS BACK UP *to the original scenery scrim and spotlight on Dr. Louise.*

(To audience again) We have a beginning . . . in the beginning. And we have an ending. And, if we're lucky, we get to do something worthwhile in the times between.

Look at these mountains. They seem to move. Did I have a mountain to climb? No, I was lucky. I simply set out to do what I wanted to do, and it was fun. I would like to preach just one last little sermon, and this I truly believe.

I don't think that 'cause I'm from eastern Kentucky I'm any more ignorant than people are in any other place in the world. I think you can do anything you want to do—if it's real and if you really want to do it. But you have to have a stimulus from someplace, and I believe you can pull it out from within yourself.

You know how you look out there and see the stars and want one? You don't get it that way—just by wanting. You have to be capable, and you have to train yourself. Be physically able and socially able to adjust to people. And listen carefully to those daggone emotions. You have to be able to get the "feel of things." Whatever those things are—religion, society, social status, family, cultural level—that's what makes you YOU. It's the soul. It's the spirit. Everybody out there has something you desire to do. You have to make your situation fit you. Evaluate it.

Now, I could never wear fancy hats and high heels. That wasn't me. Had to find that out. You can't be somebody foreign to you. I wasn't smart. I studied hard, yeah. I really believe if you work hard enough, you can make up for your own ignorance. As for me 'n Susie, all we ever wanted was for everyone to be well!
BLACKOUT. CURTAIN

[1]In 1996, Susie was given an honorary doctorate by Morehead State University.